# EXIT RAMP

# EXIT RAMP

## A SHORT CASE STUDY OF THE PROFITABILITY OF PANHANDLING

### BY

# DAVID P. SPEARS II

MADISON STREET
PUBLISHING

Paperback ISBN: 978-0-9836719-4-7
Publisher: Madison Street Publishing
1 3 5 7 9 10 8 6 4 2

*To my first political science professor at community college. He accidently created another economist with three little words: "Follow the money."*

*Also, to my first economics professor at community college. He told us not to worry about learning to read graphs. None of us were going to become economists by profession, so why bother?*

# CONTENTS

# INTRODUCTION

*"The practical uses of economic studies should never be out
of the mind of the economist, but his special business is
to study and interpret facts and to find out what are the
effects of different causes acting singly and in combination."*

–ALFRED MARSHALL

All across the highways and byways of America a common phenomenon occurs. Take any exit into a metropolitan destination, and the odds are good you will see a man standing at the street corner with a cardboard sign. The sign will tug at your heartstrings or appeal to your sense of humor; it will ultimately be a plea for charity. The goal of the man and his sign is the exchange of money.

The men—and women—who occupy the street corners go by many different names: beggars, transients, panhandlers, and bums. They don't fit into the greater American mythology; they are an unsightly blight on our land of opportunity where success is viewed as a ripe fruit just waiting to be plucked by those willing to make the effort. The bum standing at the exit ramp is often an uncomfortable reminder of failure and poverty.

I suspect that I am like the majority of drivers. I try to read the various signs while earnestly endeavoring to avoid that awkward moment of eye contact. I hate that first look where the transient gazes expectantly with sorrowful eyes. My first thought is always, "Get a job!" At the risk of sounding like an uncharitable scrooge, I can't remember ever having rolled down my window in charity. No, I always seem be the one irritably stuck behind the person with the kinder heart— while the light is green and traffic jams up.

Even though panhandlers have thus far been unable to open my wallet, they have always piqued my curiosity. Think about it: *Have you ever wondered how much a panhandler makes?* It's an interesting question. Basic economics teaches that there must be some incentive for a person to stand on a corner hat in hand. The panhandler must receive some amount of money to make the effort worthwhile, right? If he did not receive any handouts, no matter how much he was down on his luck, he would be forced to seek other means of gaining money. Intuitively, we all understand this—no one would panhandle if it did not work. And since we know panhandling does work, the question that has always nagged me is: *How well does it work?*

As this question really took hold of my economic curiosity, I started asking it in a slightly different manner: *What can a transient make per hour?* If I could compare panhandling at an exit ramp with earning a wage during the typical forty hour work week, *which would be the more profitable?*

It's easy to jump to the conclusion that someone without a job is, by default, worse off than someone gainfully employed, but how do we know this for sure? If we were to judge just by sight, then the appearance of the scrungy street souls with their tattered cardboard signs and dirty faces leads us to quick conclusions. Indeed, the question, visually, seems to answer itself.

Yet, looks can be deceiving. If panhandling, despite all appearances, can earn a man minimum wage, then can't we say that the transient at the exit ramp has the same financial opportunities as anyone else? Depending on the amount of charity received, a beggar could have the same financial means as the kid straight out of high school starting his first job.

To satisfy my growing curiosity of how much a transient makes per hour (and consequently, to find out if he makes more or less than a minimum-wage-earner), I found myself needing hard data and a way to compare incomes. The outline for this book took shape as the idea of *personally* collecting the data struck me. This case study, which grew out of the simple curiosity of how much a panhandler makes in a day, is my attempt to answer, quantitatively, the question of profitability in relation to panhandling.

With this empirical goal in mind, I decided the best course of action would be to build a little economic engine of my own. Over the summer break of my senior year at college, while double majoring in political science and economics, I put my education to good use and started collecting data on panhandling. This was my first attempt as an aspiring economist at basic quantitative analysis and social study.

What follows are the adventures I experienced while building a useable data set. The numbers and stories, the spreadsheets and anecdotes—they are all the results of my going undercover as a homeless beggar and collecting the information firsthand. This book chronicles my attempt to live up to the inspiring words of Alfred Marshall and never forget the "practical uses of economic studies." I invite all those possessed of a healthy dose of curiosity and all those unafraid of spreadsheets to join me...as I go undercover at the exit ramp.

# CHAPTER 1

# DAY ONE

*"Economics like other social life does not conform to a simple and coherent pattern. On the contrary, it often seems incoherent, inchoate and intellectually frustrating."*

–JOHN KENNETH GALBRAITH

I have always hated first days. In particular, the first day at a new job seems to be a day designed to be especially excruciating. You don't know anyone, you're unsure of what exactly you should be doing—or not doing—at any given moment. You have to ask directions just to use the bathroom. My personal nightmare is a *Groundhog Day* scenario that repeats the first day of a new job over and over and over.

The first day of my social study had the potential of being just such a memorable first day. When only a theory, going undercover as a homeless transient in the name of economic discovery is a great idea. When you have to physically go out and do it, the idea loses a certain amount of its luster. I mean, seriously—who goes out to beg for money if they don't have to? It's not exactly the normal undergraduate thing to do during one's senior summer break.

Planning ahead for the possibility that I might have misgivings, I preemptively put measures in place—just in case I tried to chicken out at the last moment. A few months prior to my start date, I strategically began telling family members about my intent to conduct this economic experiment. The responses ranged from genuine interest to accusations of mental instability. What telling people really did was create positive peer pressure. I had told everyone what I planned to do, so when it came time to do it, I could not back out—not without losing face.

The morning of July 3, 2012, I was quite glad I had taken such irregular precautions. As I got dressed and readied myself to play the part of a bum, I had a surprising case of stage fright. No one has ever accused me of being timid, but that morning I found myself conducting a classic internal dialogue: "Are you sure you really want to do this?"

It was not that I wasn't well prepared; I was. First and foremost, I had the appropriate amount of facial hair. My beard had been carefully uncultivated with about two months' worth of growth. My follicle rank was somewhere above Tony Stark's goatee but a bit below Grizzly Adams' masterpiece. I might have had the butterflies, but my beard was ready to do its duty as the focal point of my disguise. It successfully changed my face from college-educated, middle class to street-worn and weary.

The rest of my disguise was as unkempt as my beard. My old, faded army baseball cap, fraying apart in three different places, was ready to keep off the summer's heat. My T-shirt was a dirty black relic torn at the sleeves and neck. My pants (always an important part of any disguise) were tan Carhartt knock-offs that had seen considerable use in construction work and sported a softball-sized rip in the left knee. For standing all day, I wore a pair of used hiking boots, the iconic footwear of the Pacific Northwest.

Two more items rounded out my urban uniform, one mostly inconsequential and one that was vital to the nature of this study. The lesser of the two items was my well-traveled, camouflage backpack. In my Army days, it was an old tactical bag that carried spare ammo and radio batteries through the dust of Iraq. Beat-up and faded, it now bolstered the general impression of homelessness and provided a place to store my spare water and cell phone.

Besides my backpack, the other item I carried with me was my cardboard sign, the most essential item at the exit ramp. While the beard and worn out clothes served their purpose to help create the right impression, my sign was the item that would directly initiate the act of charitable giving—the very act I was keen to record. From the beginning, my sign would be a key variable and a major determinate of my overall profitability while panhandling.

## A SIGN OF THE TIMES

In the planning leading up to my first day, I gave considerable thought as to what my sign should say. In my experience there are really only two styles of begging signage: the serious and the humorous. Speaking in generalities, a beggar is either "homeless and hungry" or he is "saving up money for Kung Fu lessons because ninjas killed his parents." These categories, while they are broad, lead one to ask the obvious economic question: *Which style works best?*

This was one of the secondary questions I had hoped to

answer with my data. My original aspiration was to study both styles of signage and prove one to be more profitable than the other. I wanted to spend a full month conducting this study, splitting the time between a humorous sign and a serious sign. Regrettably, that idea ended up scrapped on the cutting room floor of life. Medical emergencies have a way of changing one's plans, especially when they involve your kid. I was forced to reduce my data collection from a month's worth of hours to two weeks.

As a result of all the medical drama, a shorter study with fewer variables seemed the way to go, and I decided to jettison the idea of two different signs. The profitability of a humorous sign in comparison to a serious sign is still a great and lingering question. It will be the first thing I return to if I pursue this topic as part of my post-graduate education. Limitations being what they were at the time, however, I chose only one style of signage—serious.

After a bit of brainstorming, I wrote the words *Iraq Vet, Anything Helps* in bold black Sharpie upon my cardboard canvass. This choice, while having the benefit of being 100% truthful, ended up causing some interesting, unintended consequences. I will explain more about this in a later chapter.

With the bold block lettering, the front of the sign looked like any other homemade sign you might see on the street corner. The back was a different story. Here my inner economist came out as I stapled a standard sized clipboard to the back of my plea for help. Pinned in the clipboard were blank worksheets with the trademark columns and rows of Excel— the perfect traps to ensnare the data I was after. And speaking of data, it was time to stop wavering and collect some.

# LOCATION, LOCATION, LOCATION

Despite my initial hesitation, I really did want to find the answers to my questions. Around 9:40 A.M. there was nothing left to do but do it. It was time to take the first step out my front door and commence this social experiment.

I had already scoped out and decided upon my destination. It had been a relatively easy choice, a variation on the "shop local" theme that is so big in Oregon. My house is conveniently located within fifteen minutes' walking distance from a busy exit ramp. I did some due diligence and drove around to different spots to compare their potential, but my local exit ramp seemed as good as any and no different from the rest. The ease of my commute became one of life's little ironies. I walked each day from the doorstep of my home to go pretend that I was homeless.

The exit ramp I used is the exit off of Interstate 205 southbound onto Highway 99 East in Oregon City, Oregon. For those unfamiliar with the area, Clackamas County has 383,857 residents and is the third most populous county in Oregon.[1] The area is divided between the urban overflow of Portland and the rural beauty of the Pacific Northwest; you can enjoy big city lights or the slopes of Mt. Hood all in the same county. I-205 cuts through the west side of Clackamas County and is one of two main freeways traveling up and down the historic Willamette valley. Any exit ramp off this busy interstate is a prime panhandling location. Travel just a

---

1   United States Census Bureau, "Clackamas, Oregon," State and County Quick Facts, U.S. Department of Commerce, http://quick-facts.census.gov/qfd/states/41/41005.html (accessed 6 July 2013).

few exits north of this location, a bit closer to Portland, and it is not uncommon to see panhandlers out daily.

I arrived at the exit ramp at 9:55 A.M., unslung my backpack, and took a look around. The layout of this exit ramp was similar to what you might expect. The exit itself consists of a long, shallow S-turn that slopes off I-205 southbound and ends in a T-intersection at Highway 99E (also called McLoughlin Boulevard at this spot).

I stood looking at three lanes of traffic coming off I-205 and turning onto 99E. The closest lane to me was a right-hand turn onto 99E northbound, while the middle and far lanes were left-hand turns onto 99E southbound into Oregon City proper. A small strip mall was located at my back with a Shari's Café being the closest building, not more than a hundred feet away.

As creature comforts go, the spot was not too shabby. I was surrounded by a few large trees and some small shrubs. It did not take long for me to learn that the trees only provided shade up until 11:00 A.M., but it is true what they say—beggars can't be choosers. There was also only a moderate amount of road trash around the spot and enough open space that I never felt cramped. In those first few seconds of looking around, I had the great feeling that I had chosen the right spot.

That euphoria fled as soon as I adjusted my sign and faced oncoming traffic. I was instantly uncomfortable. Everyone was noticeably staring at me—except for the one driver who was staring at everything *but* me. Not being one of those chemically imbalanced people who need to be the life of the party or have the constant spotlight, I found the situation more than slightly disconcerting and generally weird.

It did not help matters that my internal dialogue jumped

on the chance to remind me that I was a fraud and only faking poverty. Even though I was conducting this little charade for intellectual research, I could not shake the feeling that it was dishonest and that I had no business asking people for money. My moral compass was spinning in circles, and I dizzily suspected people could see right through my disguise. Going undercover sounds a lot easier than it really is. No wonder James Bond drinks like a fish.

The light changed to green, and the first set of cars cleared out. I started to settle down as I realized that the cars must flow. It became a small comfort that no matter how people stared at me—the evil eye, the sympathetic frown, or the indifferent nod—they could only do so for about a minute before they were on their way. The situation was uncomfortable, but it was a discomfort I could manage. The cars continued to come and go as the light changed from red to green and back again.

At 10:00 A.M. the first thing worthy of any note happened. A Clackamas County Sherriff's truck drove up to the intersection. I made eye contact, and the driver picked up his radio and started transmitting something. At that moment I had my first epiphany—I really should have checked with local ordinances to see if what I was doing was legal.

Lately, there has been a movement in many municipalities to pass restrictions against panhandling or aggressive begging. There has also been a push back as these types of ordinances are being contested as a free speech issue. Some say the conflict has the potential to reach the Supreme Court. Whether or not this will be the case, I was not particularly interested in joining any historic legal battles. My main concern was to avoid starting my study in the red thanks to a citation.

Dressed as a bum, for the first time in my life I felt close to being on the wrong side of the law.

The light mercifully turned green, and the Sheriff's truck drove on. After a few minutes of sweating it, thinking a local officer might respond, I figured I was in the clear. Nothing came from the incident, and this would hold true over the course of the study. County Deputies, Oregon City Police Officers, and State Troopers all drove by without ever stopping. As far as I know, I never broke any laws.

Cars continued to flow by, and I had no money to show for it. It did not take me long to come to the conclusion that panhandling is not exciting employment. If I were a great writer, I would think up some clever metaphor to relate just how boring it is to stand in one place unable to do anything but wait. I can think of nothing that adequately equals the mind-numbing feeling. Panhandling is just boring, boring, boring. No matter what pointless job you compare it to—maybe sitting at a desk and pushing pencils around—this job, I guarantee, is worse.

There is nothing to do but stand and watch cars come and go. You can't listen to music; headphones would spoil the disguise. You can't read a book; reading does not look the part. The only thing not boring was my internal dialogue, and that was asking me once again if I was indeed crazy for spending my free time begging. What happened next did not really help my side of the argument.

At 10:30 A.M. I watched a blind man walk past and use the crosswalk heading into Oregon City—probably walking to his job. My internal Jiminy Cricket had a field day with this. Here I was in the prime of my life using my summer vacation to beg for money, and a blind man was on his way to earn a day's wage while contributing something productive to society. Good grief! It was a sign. I should have interned at a law firm or something.

At this point I had to stoically remind myself I was doing this for a good cause—greater economic knowledge. I watched more cars come and go. I continued to talk to myself.

## MY FIRST TIME

Boredom and economic curiosity battled in my imagination as I watched car after car flow by. A rhythm soon developed, kept in time by the changing of the traffic light. I grew bolder in looking directly at drivers, determined to make a good faith effort at eye contact without aggressively staring anyone down. I did not know if there was a proper technique to panhandling, but I was giving it the old college try.

Just as the first hour rolled over, lightning struck. Right at 11:00 A.M. I received my first donation. An old minivan honked its horn from the parking lot behind me. I turned and saw a middle-aged, female driver waving me over. There was a little fence separating the lot from the street corner, so I jogged around it and up to the driver's window. I could see her rummaging through a purse, which I took as a good sign.

The woman handed me a single bill which I quickly placed in my pocket. "Sorry for your troubles. God bless," she said. "Thank you for your kindness," I replied. This would become my standard response to anyone who offered me money. With that, the transaction was complete. I walked back to my corner spot.

That first donation fulfilled every preconceived notion I had about panhandling and street charity. The woman I guessed to be in her mid-forties. By the looks of the van, she was blue collar at best. When she spoke, her words dripped with sympathy. By the tone of her voice, I knew for a fact she owned a cat, probably more than one. With my back to the parking lot, I pulled the bill out of my pocket—George Washington was staring up at me. I had my first dollar. This charitable donation fit perfectly with what I thought I already knew.

As the woman drove away, I could not suppress a smile—I had my first data point to record. I quickly angled my sign to write and filled in the six columns across my sheet: Amount, Time, Male/Female, Age, Vehicle, Race. My first entry was in the books. This study was off and running.

Things progressed rapidly after this breakthrough. Eight minutes later I got a second donation. Two women in a jeep drove up and handed me another single dollar as they waited for the light to change. I duly recorded their info after they passed by. I started to wonder if this study would show women to be the primary charitable donors. That idea was put on ice seven minutes later when my first male donor also gave me a dollar. Appearing to be of East Indian descent, he was also my first non-white donor. The next two donors were also male, one giving a dollar at 11:22 A.M. and one giving thirty-one cents at 11:34.

At 11:35 A.M. I had my second epiphany of the day—using the local exit ramp might not have been fully thought through on my part. Just after putting the thirty-one cents in my pocket, I looked up to see a familiar face. My wife's best friend was driving through the intersection with her out of town mother-in-law in tow. This is noteworthy because she was *not* one of the people I had mentioned this study to beforehand. The look on her face as she recognized me was... well, to put it in economic terms, priceless.

The eleven o'clock hour, it turned out, was making up for the boredom of the previous one. At 11:45 A.M. a female gave me five dollars. A quick mental calculation told me that, because of this donation, I had made nine dollars and thirty-one cents between 11:00 and noon. If only for a single hour, I had just proved it was possible to earn more than minimum wage.

It was not exactly time to break out the champagne, but I took great encouragement from the fact that things were starting to happen. It remained to be seen if I would make more or less than minimum wage over the course of the whole day, but I knew for the first time that I would at least be able to collect enough data to have something interesting to write about. Getting donations sure beat standing around and trying to be a clever conversationalist with myself.

The twelve o'clock hour also started off well. At 12:02 P.M. I received another dollar. In between that donation and the next, I got to play Good Samaritan as a car broke down at the light. I helped two women by pushing their car into the increasingly convenient lot behind my exit ramp. The car behind the stalled car was my next donor and gave me five dollars for my effort at 12:07. 12:15 saw two more dollars added, but after that, things slowed down until 12:50 when I received another single dollar bill.

The monetary amount and the tight concentration of donations during the eleven and twelve o'clock hours led me to start thinking that the lunch rush hour might be prime panhandling time. Of course, it was too early to say anything definitive. With nothing to compare my first lunch rush against, I had no way of knowing whether my first day was the norm or not. Despite my initial discomfort with panhandling, I began to look forward to my next day. More data would mean a better understanding of the big picture.

To round out the morning's take, I received a two dollar donation at 1:05 P.M. and five dollars at 1:18. To clear up any confusion, these donations are considered morning donations because I decided to break for lunch from 1:30 to 2:30. I chose that time as my lunch break because I hoped it would fall between the lunch and afternoon rush hours. I wanted to be out recording data during peak traffic times.

## THERE IS MORE TO LIFE THAN MONEY

The donation at 1:18 P.M. is worthy of note for more than monetary reasons. I started this study with the goal of discovering the cash-earning potential of panhandling, but I quickly learned that not all rewards come in the form of dollars and cents. Many people offered help or encouragement that transcended the simple exchange of dead presidents.

At 1:18 P.M. an SUV used the same spot as the earlier minivan to wave me over. As I approached, I noticed two women in the front seats. The passenger-side female looked to be in her seventies while the driver was more ambiguously middle-aged. The driver handed me five dollars; I responded on cue and gave my line, "Thank you for you kindness." As I started to walk away, the driver spoke up. "Hey, are you looking for work?"

I stammered a bit, not really being prepared for this question, and made an on-the-spot decision to stay in character.

I replied that I had a small part time job but that it was not enough to get by on. It was an ad-libbed half-truth. I really did work only a part time job, but I had been getting by thanks to the new 9/11 G.I. bill which provided a stipend while also paying for college. My mortgage was getting paid on time.

The driver suggested I look up a local concrete cutting company whose owner she knew personally. The company was hiring and had a preference for vets. The passenger vigorously nodded her head in agreement and gave me the stern grandma look. I thanked them for the offer, asked for the name of the company again, and said I would look into it. We then went our separate ways.

It took only half a day of being fictitiously unemployed and homeless before I was offered a job. This, quite frankly, blew me away. It was a good reminder that economic measurements and indicators don't always tell us the full story about life. A major sub-theme of this study will be revealing all the ways, aside from the handing over of spare change, that people offered assistance. I never set out to look at panhandling from this angle, but sometimes research has a way of changing your perspective. Life has a way of telling its own stories.

The job offer was not even the very first offer of help. That actually came earlier in the day, about a minute after the 11:45 A.M. donation. It was not a full-blown job offer but, in a way, it was even more heartfelt—it was an offer of help from one veteran looking out for another.

At 11:46 A.M. a truck stopped in—wait for it!—the lot behind my corner. The owner was a middle-aged man who waved me over and asked who I had served with. I duly responded with my unit and Military Occupational Specialty (or MOS). Once the ice was broken and he was assured I was indeed a legitimate veteran, he explained that he was also a vet and offered me a ride to the V.A. building or the local VFW. He wanted to get me in touch with people who could help.

At this point, I decided to explain what I was really doing. The man's act of kindness, based on our common brotherhood, deserved to be acknowledged and treated with respect. I wanted him to know why I was turning down the offer of help so as not to discourage him from helping other vets in real need.

It took some explaining, and I had to show him my clipboard before he really started to believe I was out doing a social experiment. I apologized for causing him to go out of his way under false pretenses. I could tell, by the puzzled look on his face, he was a little put off. He did not quite know what to make of someone panhandling for what sounded like a school project.

I thanked him for the offer of help and we talked a bit about common veteran experiences. After I reassured him that I was really all right, we parted ways. Even years after serving, the bond of brotherhood can cause a soldier to stop for a total stranger and drop everything to help. Such is the nature of having lived a military life.

## ONE DAY DOWN

At 2:30 P.M. I returned from my lunch break and saw no action until 2:58 when I received one dollar from a male in an unremarkable car. The next donation was also a dollar at 3:12. From there it was another long, boring spell of watching cars and inhaling exhaust fumes until 4:15 when I received forty-five cents for my troubles.

I missed a donation at 4:24 P.M. A truck driver was waving cash out his window, but I did not see it until the light turned and the truck started forward. The truck was in the second lane of traffic, and I did not feel like playing a life or death game of Frogger just to get an unspecified amount of petty cash. The donation got away, but I lived to see another day.

At 4:46 P.M. I collected my last donation of the day in the amount of three dollars. Five o'clock was my quitting time and the first day of panhandling became officially complete. In this first outing I recorded six hours of data, received sixteen monetary donations, and was offered assistance twice. I walked home, sat at my desk, and looked over the results.

Tallying my day's work revealed that nine females and seven males had contributed. My total haul for the day was $30.76, which breaks down to an hourly average of $5.13 per hour. While I had failed to make minimum wage for the day, I was anything but discouraged.

I interpreted the first day's results as a mixed signal. If you isolate the eleven to one o'clock time period, I averaged $9.15 per hour. This proved it was indeed *possible* to make more than minimum wage, if only for two hours on a single day. Which result would win out throughout the course of the study—a daily average plodding in below minimum wage or the potential of the rush period pushing me triumphantly above it? The answer remained to be seen.

I needed more data like an alcoholic needs another whisky. Was my first day panhandling a good or a bad one? I had a single enigmatic piece of an economic jigsaw puzzle. Sitting in my study, I knew only one thing for sure—by the end of my panhandling project I was going to have good stories and hard data. I had collected enough information that first day to trust that an economic map would indeed emerge as I continued my investigation. I was onto something—I just had to panhandle for seventy-four more hours to find out what.

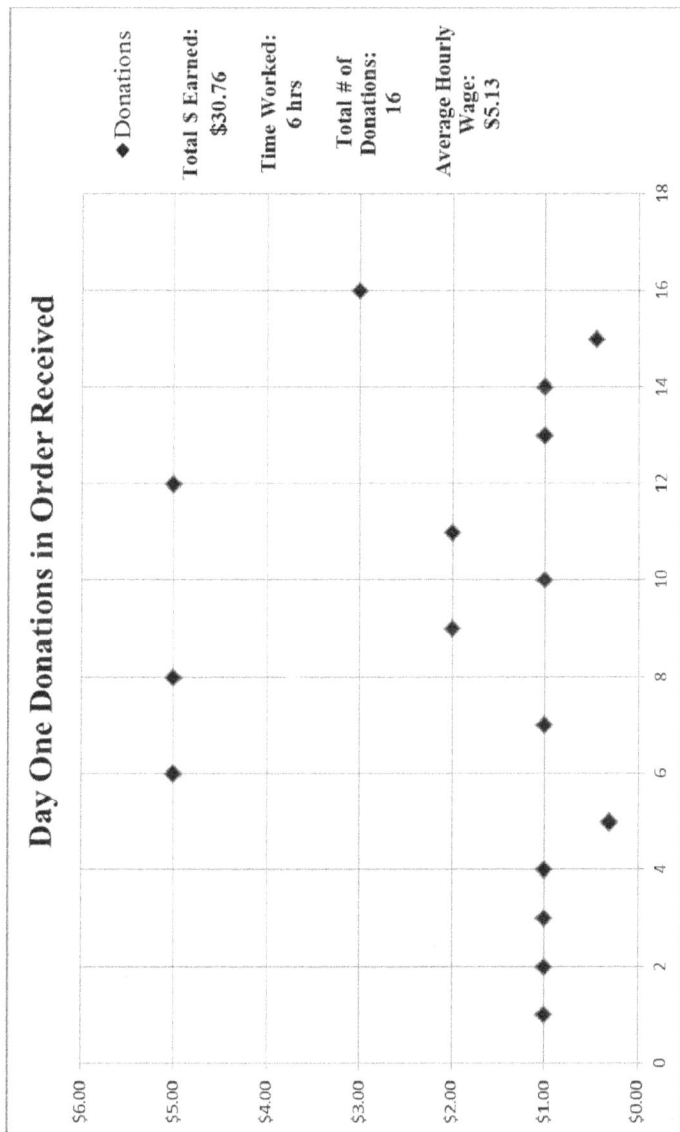

*Figure 1: Day One - Donations*

# CHAPTER 2

# LOW HANGING FRUIT

*"You know, it's said that an economist is the only
professional who sees something working in practice
and then seriously wonders if it works in theory."*

–RONALD REAGAN

My second day panhandling jumped out of the starting
blocks at a quicker pace than my first. Within a minute
of dropping my backpack and "clocking in," a black mustang
executed a sharp lane change and drove up to where I was
standing. I received a twenty dollar bill, my first donation of
that denomination. It was a stupendous start to the day. Mentally, the next two hours of standing around had already been
paid for. After this initial excitement, however, the day settled down to a more familiar pattern—stretches of boredom
broken up by moments of random kindness.

I am not going to write the majority of this book as a linear
retelling of each day, hour by hour and donation by donation.
That would be, frankly, as boring to write as it would be to
read—and then, and then, and then *ad nauseam*.

I will return to a summary account of my second day later,

but for now, let's start to unpack the data I recorded by topic. Organizing the data topically will allow us to more easily see patterns and to better draw conclusions. The stories of how I collected the data will fall into place as we go, but for now the numbers will dominate the narrative.

## THE HIGHEST DONATION, THE LOWEST DONATION

After the publication of this study, when I get invited to swank cocktail parties with rock stars and famous economists, I am sure one of the first questions I will be asked by a supermodel is, *"What was the largest amount of money any one person gave you?"* As questions go, it's as good a place to start as any, and it might be the lowest hanging fruit of my study.

The largest donation I received came rather early on, in the middle of my third day, on July 11. It was the fourth donation of the day, received at 11:47 A.M. A minivan pulled into the lot behind my corner. Distracted by the flow of cars at the street corner, I did not even notice the parked vehicle until the middle-aged female driver walked around the fence and approached me. Thinking back on the encounter, I should have realized that the driver approaching me was the first clue that something was different. Most people, in my limited experience of panhandling, will call the man with the cardboard sign over to their vehicle as they stay safely inside. For unknown reasons, this woman was different.

I watched her as she closed the distance to hand me a single bill. As appearances go, there was nothing distinctive about her. She could have been the sister of cat lady for all I knew. "God bless you and thank you for your service," she said as she handed me the bill. At that very moment, I knew intuitively that something was up.

I glanced down and recognized a one followed by two zeros. Subconsciously, I had already put two and two together. A hundred dollar bill has a very different tactile feel from the more commonly used one dollar bill.

I did a double take to see what kind of person hands out hundred dollar bills to street bums. I also managed to weakly mumble, "Thank you. Thank you for your kindness."

She looked me squarely in the eyes, smiled, and then, as simple as that, went back to her van. I stood there for a moment, more or less dumbfounded that someone had just given me a hundred dollar bill. It qualified as a lot of money even by my suburban, middle-class, non-panhandling standards.

To tell you the truth, I felt incredibly guilty about it. She did not look like someone affluent enough to treat a hundred dollars like it was just pocket change. I felt like someone had punched me in the stomach. This woman's generosity had impelled her to give me, a total stranger, a hundred dollars. It was both flattering and frightening—I never felt more like a scam artist than I did at that moment. At that moment I promised myself I would pass along this generosity and "pay it forward." I also pledged not to easily forget this one person's testament to the great kindness and benevolence still embedded in American culture.

On the flip side, there is also the matter of my smallest donation recorded. I received it on the eighth day panhandling, August 13. By odd coincidence it happened at almost the same time of day that I received my largest donation. At 11:41 a beater Honda pulled up in the closest lane at the intersection.

The beater held five occupants who were collectively a sight to see—a group of sixteen-year-olds who looked like eleventeen year olds. In what was obviously a case of someone taking Avril Lavigne's "Skater Boy" song a little too seriously, they were all dressed head to foot in clothes that screamed skater-punk. They were walking, talking, barely-old-enough-to-drive billboard signs for Zumiez.

When the passenger rolled down his window, I was taken by surprise. I had not expected them to be the Bill and Melinda Gates type. I approached the car with due caution. They looked more than capable of throwing a flaming bag of poo out the window—or whatever else is popular with prank-sters these days. I thought discretion might be the order of the day.

Despite my uncharitable attempts to stereotype them, the passenger was indeed offering some loose change in charitable kindness. Normally, I can't count loose change in front of the donor without being obvious and rude. I stuff it in one of my many pockets and tally it up at the end of the day. In this par-ticular case, the change amounted to four pennies. I was not going to need to count this handful later. "Thanks," I said. At least it was not an egging.

"Sorry, dude," said the kid in the passenger seat. "It's all I could find." It was genuine; he was not being a smart ass. I laughed and said it was all good, and then I thanked him again—this time sincerely—for his kindness.

While the light remained red, I watched the Junior Philan-thropist look around the car for more change. He found another handful of coins, but destiny stepped in and decided it did not belong in my pocket—well, maybe it was his driver who decided that. As I started to return to the car for the second handful of change, the light turned green. The driver, assumedly having a difference of opinion with his passenger about charity and bums, punched the gas petal. Before I could collect part two of the donation, the Honda's tires squealed and the car shot forward. I stood there and smiled. Sometimes a testament to our culture's innate kindness comes in the form of four cents.

## THE MOST PROFITABLE DAY, THE LEAST PROFITABLE

Along with the high and low single donations, we can also look at the highest daily haul and the lowest—or, to put it another way, the most and least profitable days. These two days can be thought of as the bookends of my research. They give the range of what is possible.

If you have already guessed that the third day was my best day, then you are correct. Getting a hundred dollars does wonders for hourly income averages. With the help of that Benjamin, my average hourly wage on the third day topped out as $24.63 per hour for the 6.75 hours I spent panhandling.

Let that sink in for a moment.

I earned close to three times Oregon's minimum wage. On that one day, I could honestly say it was *three times* more profitable for me to panhandle than to work an entry level job. Those 6.75 hours were over twice as profitable as the eight hour day I had worked at my previous summer job—one of those things that make you go hmm....

With the hundred dollar donation in play, during the eleven to one o'clock time span I collected $128.25 in donations. Over those two short but sweet hours, I earned a whopping $64.13 per hour. If you want to be a stickler and discount the hundred dollars as an unrealistic outlier, I still made a respectable $14.13 per hour—still setting me quite comfortably above minimum wage. By the third day, my hypothesis that the lunch rush was the sweet spot of panhandling—the prime time to make a buck—was being confirmed.

Of course, not all my days were as equally successful as the third day. This was the high end of my spectrum, and I received that hundred spot only once. We also need to consider the matter of my least profitable day. It is important, not so much because of the small amount earned, but because of the interesting implications it hints at.

Once I completed my study and looked over all the data, I was a bit surprised. My least profitable day was in fact my *first* day panhandling. As I related earlier, I had earned a wage of $5.13 per hour. This was the lowest average hourly wage of any day in the whole study.

What this implies is fascinating—and a bit controversial, even in my own mind. Earning the least amount on my first day seems to imply that there is a learning curve to the profession of panhandling. A job posting on Craigslist for panhandling might say, "DOE"—pay is "depending on experience." In other words, what I think the numbers are showing is that my inexperience on the first day—my jitters, my lack of eye contact, my general body language—was directly responsible for my lowest daily wage. If this is true, it implies that there is a certain skill set to panhandling. The fact that my daily average wage consistently improved over the first three days also lends some credence to this possibility.

I don't want to go overboard with this line of thought. My study is just too small to say definitively if the first day was indeed a sign that experience counts in panhandling just as it does in any other profession. It could be equally true that the first day was just a statistical fluke.

To really find out the truth of the matter, I would need to reproduce this study with other actors who also started panhandling for the first time. If their first days showed a similar tendency to be the least profitable, we might be able to draw some concrete conclusions. As it is, I can say this with confidence: there is, at the very least, an *appearance* of a connection between experience and profitability in panhandling.

What you can take away from all this is your first clue. You now know my lowest daily hourly earnings came in at $5.13 per hour and my highest came in at $24.63 per hour. That accounts for two out of the twelve days or 12.75 out of 80 hours. Only counting 16% of the time spent panhandling, this averages out to an hourly wage of $14.88. The remaining days fall somewhere between the high and low benchmarks, and the real question is: *Which day will be more normative—the first day or the third day?* The remaining 84% of this study will determine if I earn above or below minimum wage.

## AS THE DAYS GO BY

Though I have given you some hints as to how my third day went, the last place I left you—chronologically speaking—was at the beginning of day two. The second day stands out for two reasons: it was the first day I earned over minimum wage, and I was only able to work 4.5 hours because...the competition stole my spot.

First off, my daily hourly wage for the second day ended at $10.21. This was, in large part, thanks to the larger donations of twenty dollars at 9:15 A.M., five dollars at 9:19, ten dollars at 11:40, and five dollars at 12:43 P.M. The day was busy beyond the money as well. At 11:50 and 12:15, two different veterans stopped to offer help as I will relate in the next chapter.

The second day was an exciting but inconclusive day. Although I had averaged above minimum wage, I could not fully trust the results. Why? Because I only worked 4.5 hours. My day was cut short by circumstances beyond my control. This led to some feelings of doubt—if I had worked six or seven hours, would my average have slipped?

The event beyond my control happened right as I came back from lunch. A female of middle age and skinny build was standing with her own sign on my corner. My spot had been taken while I was away.

This did not come as a complete surprise. I had first seen the woman earlier in the day around 10:30 A.M. She had walked by, mumbling something to the effect that I had taken her spot. I just shrugged, and she kept on walking. I watched as she moved to the onramp at the other side of the highway to set up shop.

Despite her claim, I sincerely doubted that she had any sort of squatter's rights to this particular exit. I had scoped out the spot several times (after all, it's an exit ramp I drive frequently), and I had never seen either her or any other panhandler consistently use it. I had done my homework, and I had picked the spot knowing full well I was not taking it from someone else.

The first time I saw her it raised in my mind an interesting question. When it comes to panhandling locations, does interest beget interest? Economics 101 teaches that a firm's profit will act as a signal for other firms to enter the market. Apparently, this economic principle holds true for panhandlers just as much as it does for multi-national corporations.

By lunchtime on the second day, the competition had disappeared, and so I counted it safe to head home for a sandwich and the modern convenience of indoor plumbing. By the time I returned, the female had swooped into my spot, and I had been pushed out of my prime real estate.

Now, if I had wanted to stay in character, I am sure I could have scared her off and defended my turf. But as much as I wanted to continue gathering data, yelling at a homeless woman was never really a consideration—I was not that committed to my charade. I called it a day and headed home, only logging 4.5 hours worked.

I was not really depending on my earnings, so she could have my spot for the afternoon. It all worked out. The next day she was nowhere to be found, and I never saw her again.

The monetary success of the following day, the third day, has by now been well established. Besides the money, I also received a cigarette and a Baptist church invitation—mind you, not from the same person. Although the day was all about the Benjamin, it actually started with someone giving me not money but a homeless packet full of hygiene goods. What comes in a homeless hygiene packet you ask? Well, that's just what we'll get to next....

**Average Hourly Wage for First Three Days Panhandling**

| | | |
|---|---|---|
| Day 1 | $5.13 | |
| Day 2 | $10.21 | |
| Day 3 | $24.63 | |

$0.00 — $5.00 — $10.00 — $15.00 — $20.00 — $25.00 — $30.00

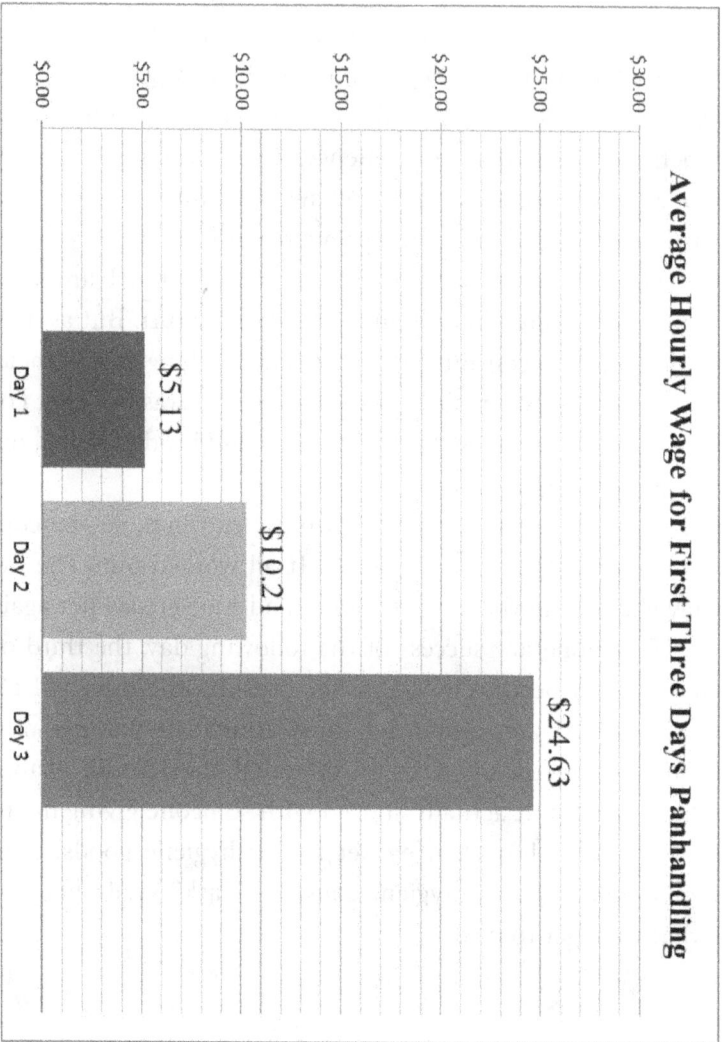

*Figure 2: Days One through Three - Averages*

# CHAPTER 3

# GOODS AND
# SERVICES

*"There's no such thing as a free lunch."*

–MILTON FRIEDMAN

O kay, I admit it—when I first started this study I only thought about the money. I wanted to find out how much of it I could make. I narrowly defined my objectives around a monetary framework, and I began thinking in almost purely classical economic terms. I thought of panhandling as simply an exchange of money that I could quantify. Once properly quantified, I would draw some graphs, make some conclusions, and then pen this book. Everything else outside my simple model could be assumed away—*"ceteris paribus."*

Now, you'd think with my liberal arts education I would have remembered life can't be reduced as neatly as all that. As I gained experience at the exit ramp, I made a significant and unexpected discovery. Out at the corner I found a shadow economy operating in and around the monetary one. People were being charitable with more than just their money.

I started this study measuring pennies, quarters, and

dollars; I ended this study measuring charity more broadly. Along with dollars, I also had to account for McChicken sandwiches, canned ravioli, and toothpaste. As I started to fully appreciate that an additional economy of goods and services existed, I understood that it would have its own story to tell about the exit ramp. This chapter is that story.

## IT IS BETTER TO RECEIVE THAN TO GIVE

August 16 was my tenth day panhandling, and it was stupid hot outside. Okay, not Arabian desert or Texas hot, but still plenty hot for mild-mannered Oregon. The temperature for the day peaked at 97 degrees, and I spent a good seven hours getting blinded by the glare of windshields. Twenty-five minutes before I quit for the day, I was once again astonished by a stranger's generosity.

I was standing my post—mentally counting down the seconds until I could leave—when out of the corner of my eye I noticed a feminine group heading my way from the Shari's. The group consisted of a middle-aged woman with a girl on either side. The girls looked anywhere from six to eight years old. The adult female was carrying a takeout bag from Shari's.

I initially assumed that the group was heading across the intersection and wanted nothing to do with me. As they rounded the fence, however, they surprised me by turning my way instead of stopping at the crosswalk. The woman—already different than most people in bringing children to meet me—really stood out being dressed in nurse's scrubs. As they approached, my curiosity was piqued to see what would come of this encounter.

"I saw you standing out here and wanted to get something for you," the woman said. She handed me the bag she was carrying and slipped me a ten dollar bill along with it. Inside the bag was a takeout box which I later discovered held a club sandwich and fries. "Thank you," I said and told her how much it meant to me to have someone be so kind.

The nurse seemed genuinely pleased to be doing a good deed and gave me a big smile—not the "I feel so sorry for you" pout that some people have when they give. I got the distinct feeling that this nurse's act of kindness was also being used as a teaching moment. I can't prove it, but the way the nurse brought the two little girls over to the exit ramp felt deliberate. The way she held their hands on the return trip to the Shari's parking lot betrayed the care of someone actively involved. Those girls were not told how to be kind—they were shown.

The experience also taught *me* something as well. I understood from this exchange, more than any other, that the story of the exit ramp would not be complete if I only wrote about the ten dollars the nurse gave me, while leaving out the club sandwich with all the fixings. Just because it fell outside my original goal of the study—to calculate an average hourly wage for panhandling—the club sandwich should not be overlooked. The day by day breakdown of goods I received—and the kindness behind those gifts—proves just as interesting as the tally of dollars and cents.

On day one I received a box of chocolate candies from a female—I do not think there were any romantic feelings behind the gift. Day two proved to be cash only.

On day three I received a homeless care package at 9:55 A.M., a Baptist church invitation flyer at 3:27 P.M., and a very non-Baptist cigarette at 3:54. The cigarette came from an extremely "Portland" looking female, who by all appearances probably had less money than I did at the moment but still found a way to be kind.

On day four I received another cigarette at 12:51 P.M.—I seriously thought I might need to take up smoking just to properly appreciate all the cancer sticks I was receiving. At 3:24 I received a Powerade drink from a female truck driver. This is noteworthy—no, not because it was the first time I had ever seen a female truck driver, but because it was the first time a truck driver of either sex had given me anything. I was starting to think truckers were immune to panhandlers until this transaction. At 4:04 I was given a McDonald's gift card by a kind elderly couple.

Day five started with a pack of beef jerky at 11:49 A.M. I was also given bottled water at 12:20 P.M. and a fruit smoothie, of all things, at 1:14.

Day six was a slow day. I only received a banana at 12:51 P.M. and a can of beans at 3:10—not that I would actually ever consume a can of beans, even if I really were homeless. Let's be honest here.

Day seven, on the other hand, was my best day in terms of items received. At 10:10 A.M. I received a coupon for a free Chalupa from Taco Bell, and at 10:40 I received candy (which I did *not* eat thanks to the remembered warnings of my mother). At 11:17 it was a doughnut followed by half of a homemade sandwich. At 4:03 P.M. a driver offered to buy me a meal, but I turned down the offer in the interests of continuing my research. This worked out for the best because at 4:06 a driver handed me a beer bottle—clearly, a superior good to the hypothetical meal. At 4:40 I got a packet of crackers to go with the beer.

The beer definitely stands out as the most interesting thing I received during this whole study. I try not to think too much about how the driver was able to hand me a single beer—open container laws, I believe, frown on such things. The beer itself was the exact color of urine and appeared to be of the "value" variety of alcohol. I decided that if I actually drank the beer I would have officially gone deep undercover—maybe too deep. There is a line to just how far I was willing to go in the name of research.

On day eight I received a cookie at 11:07 A.M. and a bean burrito at 12:49 P.M. (If there's anything worse than beans, it's beans wrapped up in an otherwise perfectly good tortilla.)

On day nine I received my second McDonald's gift card at 12:50 P.M., an otherwise slow day for receiving goods.

On day ten, the day I received the club sandwich from the nurse, I also received a soda at 3:40 P.M., bottled water at 3:51, Gatorade at 5:20 and a Frappuccino at 5:48. As I said, it was hot outside; people responded in kind.

My day eleven lunch was provided at 1:14 P.M. when a passerby gave me his spare McChicken sandwich. At 3:39 I received a lemonade drink. At 4:15 I received my second home-less packet, and at 5:00 I accepted candy from a stranger—but again I never ate it.

My last day out panhandling I received a packaged Rice Krispie treat at 9:46 A.M. and a can of ravioli at 9:51. The third and final homeless packet came at 1:57 P.M. and a bottle of water at 2:50. At 3:39 a driver gave me her Arby's fries. Less than a minute later came the very last item I collected at the exit ramp—a Gatorade.

My apologies if that list was somewhat tedious to read. I wanted to share a complete picture of all the non-cash items

I collected at the exit ramp. Even if you only skimmed the list, it should be obvious that food made up the majority of items I received—the notable exceptions being the homeless care packages which I will get to shortly. While some of the food, like the can of ravioli, seemed particularly planned out in advance, I found a lot of the charitable giving done in an ad hoc fashion. People split their lunches with me.

I must admit I was surprised by the number of times people would see me and impulsively share whatever they had on hand. When I received the packet of beef jerky, it was from a male driver who must have originally bought the packet for himself. The driver picked it up off his empty passenger seat and threw it out to me. I did not record the numbers analytically, but I can safely say the majority of the food I received was given in this way.

A minority of the items were the product of more premeditated charity. The nurse clearly planned what she was doing when she went out of her way to buy me a meal. The homeless packets also required some planning to put together. If you have never heard of premade homeless care packages, let me take a minute to explain what was in each.

The first care package I received was a hygiene kit. It was built by Portland Area Seventh Day Baptist Church. In the packet was a crocheted cross bookmark and a few paragraphs explaining their beliefs. The rest of the packet consisted of a blue washcloth, a packet of tissues, a travel size Colgate toothpaste and toothbrush combo, a bar of soap in a plastic soap case, two Gillette disposable safety razors, a pair of white socks, hand sanitizer, a 3 oz. travel shampoo bottle, a five dollar Subway gift card, and a small booklet called *Living Water: The*

*Gospel of John with Notes.* This was all in a small green reusable cloth bag printed with the words "Grace—it's amazing."

The other two homeless care packages focused more on food than hygiene. The second of the three I received was filled with: an individual bag of Cheetos, a can of Brunswick Tuna Salad, a bottled water, two peanut butter cracker packets, a cheese cracker packet, a strawberry Nutri-Grain cereal bar, a packet of Quaker instant oatmeal, a packet of chicken Top Ramen, a paper cup for hot beverages, and finally one set of plastic silverware and a napkin. This packet also came with a note: "Prepared for you with love by the Clarkes United Methodist Church in Mulino, OR. Inspired by the Father's Heart Street Mission."

The third and final package, which I can only assume represents secular charity as it came without any notes from a religious organization, consisted of: a can of ravioli, a Tree Top apple sauce single, an Alpine apple cider single, a cheese cracker packet, a Nutri-grain cereal bar (apple-cinnamon this time), a bottled water, and again a paper cup with silverware and a napkin.

We might be getting into the weeds with this much detail, but all this is to demonstrate the strong undercurrent of generosity that still exist in our culture—evident in both the well thought out gifts and the spur of the moment charity I recorded at the exit ramp. The number of items I received and the frequency with which they were given is ample proof of the kindheartedness of strangers.

Of course, as an aspiring economist I couldn't help but want to further quantify and put a price on such charity. With a little price checking at my local Fred Meyer and Target, I roughly estimated the cost of each homeless packet. Package number one came out as costing $15.71, package number two as $5.12, and package number three as a mere $2.78. I also estimated the prices of every other item I received and added them to the value of the care packages, bringing my total to $85.63. This is the loosely estimated total value of all goods I received at the exit ramp.

## A HELPING HAND

What is harder to price, the other topic of this chapter, are the services I received at the exit ramp. While most people offered money or goods, a few individuals offered help. This help was in the form of anything from a free ride to Labor Ready to suggestions on how to get assistance from Veterans' Affairs. These acts of kindness don't show up in my final accounting, but, had I been in real need, these offers of help would have been my most valuable acquisitions.

To be exact, there were fourteen people who offered help: two the first day, two the second, one the third, three the fifth, one the sixth, two the eighth, one the ninth, one the tenth, and one last offer of help on the twelfth and final day. The services these people offered divided into two general categories: offers of work and offers of veteran assistance.

This is where, more than in any other area, the unintended consequence of using my veteran status shows up in this study. Six of the fourteen people stopping to help were fellow veterans taking the time to ask questions and offer their assistance. These encounters with veterans were the unexpected stories of my study—some are uplifting, some are cautionary.

One archetypal example happened on the second day at 1:10 P.M. The encounter started like so many of my transactions at the exit ramp as a man parked his pickup truck in the lot behind me and waved me over to talk. He got out of the truck—twenty-something, clean cut, and athletic, in the skinny wide receiver sort of way. The back of his pickup truck was crammed full of boxes and duffle bags.

The start of the conversation confirmed what my intuition had already guessed—this was a veteran stopping to offer help. He was a marine who had driven all the way from somewhere in the Midwest. On terminal leave, he was new in town and on his way to get plugged in with Oregon's Veterans' Affairs office. When he saw me, his first thought was to offer me a ride along with him to the V.A., a place where he was sure someone could do something to help.

He was a total stranger, from a different branch of the military, from a different part of the country, with his own set of problems. He was a total stranger—but he still stopped to help because we shared one thing in common. Shakespeare wrote about a band of brothers, but I wonder if he ever truly experienced it firsthand. Sometimes the strongest of bonds simply shows up as the unheroic offer of a free ride.

Being a veteran is a claim I would not recommend faking. Not all veterans were as free with their charity as my first example. On the eighth day of my study, I ran into a vet who took a slightly different approach. His story is the cautionary tale for anyone who wants to imitate my signage without the experience to back it up.

At 12:03 P.M. a short man in a well-worn baseball cap advanced toward me from the parking lot and opened up a rapid fire conversation.

"What branch where you in?"

"Army."

"What was your MOS?"

"11-Bravo."

"Where did you go to basic training and with what unit?"

"Uh...Fort Benning, Georgia, and...1-19th Infantry."

He never once broke eye contact during the interrogation, and only with my last answer did he relax a bit. I could visibly see him come to the conclusion that I was indeed a veteran as my sign indicated.

What he said next revealed the dire consequences that would have awaited me had I not known the right answers. "I was a Ranger in the Army and I stopped to either punch you in the face or give you twenty bucks."

He handed me a twenty and then he left.

I have no doubt he would have punched me too, had I proved to be a fraud. Rangers are that way—they are wound up a bit tight. He was not ungenerous, but if he hadn't received positive proof that I was the real deal, this encounter would have ended up very differently. This book is not written as a panhandling "how-to" manual, but I highly recommend *not* using a fake veteran's sign. You might meet a Ranger yourself one day.

I was always surprised and humbled when people stopped to offer me help, whether it was a ride to the V.A. or simply news of charitable organizations close by which could provide me with a bed and a meal. At the exit ramp I was offered work, help with finding a job, and free meals by total strangers. I can't easily assign a monetary value to each service I was offered, and I have no way of knowing if offers of work would have panned out. Nevertheless, I hope one can still appreciate such generosity even when it is not cash or goods.

I want to end this chapter with one more story that might

be the most comprehensive example of kindness I experienced at the exit ramp. At 10:33 A.M. on the ninth day of this study, an SUV parked in the Shari's lot and honked. I ran around the fence per usual and saw two men had climbed out of the truck to meet me halfway. One man was middle-aged and one was elderly—in his sixties maybe. The younger of the two handed me a ten dollar bill and then something else—a business card.

As I looked the card over, the man explained that he was a veterans' employment caseworker out of Vancouver, Washington. Even though I was not in his district, he knew ways to aid me in finding employment, and he had contacts in the Oregon City area. He was unexpectedly enthusiastic and encouraging. The elderly man, who was his father, also added admonishments to the conversation here and there. In a word, they both seemed very genuine.

I was, internally, on the horns of a dilemma as they earnestly offered me a hand up. I wanted to stay undercover and see where this was going, but at the same time I knew I was not going to accept any of the help they offered. I was also somewhat of a chicken. The two men were so animated in their offers of help that I did not want to admit to them that I had, in an indirect way, tricked them—I was not in need of employment or shelter.

Using the excuse that discretion is the better part of valor, I kept to my act and played my part. The caseworker gave me one final encouragement to call or email him that very evening so he could help. I thanked him for the assistance and then they left.

Once back at my corner, I immediately regretted my deception. This feeling only grew worse later in the day when the elderly man again drove by my spot. He did not stop but he did make eye contact and shout out the window, "Make sure you call my son and get yourself some help!"

I was offered help fourteen times in this study, but this father and son were by far the most ardent and indefatigable Good Samaritans I met while at the exit ramp. They both had the desire to help and the means to do so.

What I appreciated about their charity was not only the spirit in which it was given but also the fullness of it. I received a modest amount of money for my perceived immediate needs, but it was given in the context of relationship. The men introduced themselves and offered a more lasting charity aimed at changing the circumstances of my implied situation.

Now, one could be cynical and argue that it was just the caseworker's job to help, but such a statement would be a reductionist's inaccuracy, a small, distorted interpretation of what actually happened—similar to the mistake of reducing charity only to a monetary value. I was not in the man's work district, and he had no obligation to stop. He went above and beyond the duties of his employment to offer me help. That counts for a lot in my book.

In the next chapters we will be getting back to the numbers, but it is essential to remember there is always a human story behind them. The numbers are important, but they must never be seen as the whole story. Economics is the study of human action, not mathematic formula. I was reminded of this every time I pocketed another cigarette or took the tomatoes off a free Shari's club sandwich.

# CHAPTER 4

# PANHANDLING AND SEX...ER... GENDER

*"Men are from Earth, women are from Earth. Deal with it."*

–GEORGE CARLIN

Every time a group of people get together to play Pictionary, there is always that one person who suggests the teams be divided by male and female. There is also that other person who is always offended by such a suggestion. Even when just playing games, it can be controversial to imply there is a difference between the sexes—it is as equally controversial to say there is *no* difference between the sexes. Naturally then, this is what makes dividing economic data by gender so much fun. Men and women have always sought to compare themselves to the opposite sex—and then argue about the results. Who am I not to oblige?

In statistics, gender makes a perfect binary variable. You are either male or you are not; you are either female or not. The economics of this distinction is easy even for an amateur like myself. Numbers divided by gender lead down some easy avenues of inquiry without the need for a complex formula. It's not hard to say if women gave me money more times than men did, or if men averaged a higher amount per donation than the women. Interpreting what the results mean in the big picture of things is always the challenging part. I will leave that, and the inherent danger of sexism, mostly to the reader.

That's not to say when I began this study I didn't come equipped with my own preconceptions and biases about what the results would illuminate regarding gender. My own belief was that women would donate a considerable amount more, in frequency and quantity, than men would. In my mind, I equated the fairer sex with being more generous. As with many things in life, I easily convinced myself of the soundness of my own reasoning, and I assumed I knew how things would play out.

Before starting the study, I was surprised to learn that my wife and some of our friends had an opposite preconception. They believed women would be less willing to interact with a scruffy looking stranger, and, therefore, women would donate less than men. They put a heavier weight on the "stranger danger" feelings that many women have.

This difference of preconceptions highlights one of the things I have grown to love about the study of economics. It can, at its best, allow us to quantitatively examine our own biases. By asking quantitative questions, one is able to find quantitative answers, and these answers help change how we perceive life around us. I started this study with little more than self-reinforced biases, but in the process of collecting quantitative data, I was forced to adjust my preconceptions to align with what actually occurred.

Over the course of the 80 hours panhandling, I received a set amount of donations. I duly recorded the gender of each donor, whether male or female. The number of donations given by each category was surprisingly close. 53% of all monetary donations came from males, and 47% came from females. Much to the pleasure of my wife, this almost fifty-fifty split, leaning slightly in favor of males, pretty much trashed my working theory that women were more likely to donate to a panhandler. At the same time, we are only talking about a 3% advantage with a fairly small data sample. Females didn't exactly shy away from charitable giving either, and I count these results close enough for a draw.

This close of a split in the results tickled my curiosity about the overall population from which I was taking my sample. Could the higher donation count by men just be a reflection of a higher male to female ratio in the general population of Oregon or, more narrowly, the population of Clackamas County? Not according to the 2012 U.S. Census. Females make up 50.5% of the population in greater Oregon and 50.7% of the population in Clackamas.[2] If anything, gender demographics give a slim advantage to women.

Maybe state-wide and county-wide gender demographics are too broad to address this issue. What if we only count the licensed drivers? They were the ones driving by my cardboard sign, right? Are there, perhaps, more male drivers in Oregon than female drivers? Here, after some digging (thanks, Google), I turned to the U.S. Department of Transportation's Federal Highway Administration and their Office of Highway

---

2  Ibid.

Policy Information.[3] According to the 2010 numbers, men make up 49.87% of licensed drivers in Oregon and women 50.13%. Again, the numbers, while basically even, still give the slightest of edges to the women. All other things being equal, the demographics lead one to expect that the number of donations from women would, in some small measure, exceed the number of donations from men.

There is no clear, obvious answer as to why men donated a little more often than the women did over the course of my study. The minute gap between each gender's donation numbers matches the general closeness we find in the greater demographics. Again, the problem of having a small sample rears its ugly statistical head. Men leading the donation numbers could again be nothing more than a statistical fluke.

With only one short study under my belt, I don't have any evidence that my results are not simple coincidence. If I retook my sample, I suspect I might just as likely end up with a few more donations from women than from men. So much for a ground breaking economic discovery in gender differences and charitable giving....

But the *number* of donations given by each gender is not the whole story in this battle between the sexes. It is also revealing to look at the average *amount* given by each gender. Looking at gender and charity from this angle, we actually find a reversal. The women, who as we have already established gave less often, actually gave *more* by amount. The

---

3   Office of Highway Policy Information, "Highway Statistics 2010: Licensed Drivers by Sex and Ratio to Population – 2010," U.S. Department of Transportation: Federal Highway Administration, http://www.fhwa.dot.gov/policyinformation/statistics/2010/dl1c. cfm (accessed 6 July 2013).

average woman's donation amounted to $5.12. The average man's donation amounted to $4.40. Women averaged 72 cents more per donation than their counterparts did. Can we chalk this up as a win for Team Woman?

Not so fast. We still have that little issue of the one hundred dollar bill that could be considered an outlier. That single donation is the fulcrum upon which the averages swing. Take away that one jackpot transaction and the average woman's donation drops to $4.02. Without the Benjamin, women averaged 38 cents *less* than men. Interesting, no?

Personally, I count the hundred dollar bill as fair game because it really did happen during the scope of this study and therefore should be used in all calculations. I am intellectually open, however, to any male chauvinist who wants to argue that the hundred dollar bill really should be discounted as an outlier because its occurrence is, presumably, so rare. I leave you, dear reader, to choose your own side. You can agree with the chauvinist and discount the hundred or join me and the feminists and count women as the more generous by dollar amount.

What I found to be unequivocal, but surprising, was the high average of *all* the donations, whether from men or women. When I started this study, I supposed I would be gathering a lot of spare change from unused ashtrays. While I did receive spare change on occasion and a lot of single dollar bills, I also received dollar bills in groups of two, threes, and fives. The occasional twenty didn't hurt the averages either.

I will divulge the complete results of income later, but I hope it is already becoming clear that my experience was not primarily one of receiving inconsequential leftover change. I received a real and significant amount of charity from both men and women.

This outpouring of charity stuck with me long after I finished calculating the daily takes. I have related these experiences of receiving donations in statistical terms, but there is also a human aspect that should never be forgotten. This study is not just about the economics of panhandling told in abstract mathematics—it is also a tale of the people behind the numbers.

## MR. GRAY BEARD AND MS. HEPBURN

As male donors go, one stands out in my mind as a prime example of what I experienced on the corner. On the fifth day, August 3, at 1:20 P.M. a minivan once again parked behind me in the Shari's lot and honked at me to come over. By this time I had the routine down pat.

The man looked to be in his mid-40's or early 50's with gray hair and a matching well-trimmed gray beard, but what set him apart in my memory more than a physical description was the conversation he initiated. As I came up to the window, he did not just hand me cash. "How are you doing?" he asked. With these words, he sought a connection beyond a simple money exchange. I replied that I was trying to get by but that it was hard—true enough whether homeless on the street corner or going to college at age 32 with three kids and a mortgage.

"I saw you and I wanted to stop," he said, in a kind and encouraging voice. "I just received a commission bonus at work, and I have been praying about how to use it. When I saw you, I knew what I wanted to do." As he handed me a twenty dollar bill, he continued with more personal encouragement. The man, who I like to think of as Mr. Gray Beard, explained the link between his generosity and his faith. He saw only a small distance between his situation with a job and my situation without. The only reason he was able to be any different was because he took each day one step at a time and put his faith in Jesus. He said it was really the only thing anyone could do, and he hoped I would find the same peace that he had found.

It was a more sincere conversation than I can convey in relating it secondhand. His statements never felt preachy or Pollyannaish—they were the pure, heartfelt expressions of concern from a man who understood someone else's need.

This was a memorable experience for me because it stood in stark contrast to my daily digest of news media. As a political scientist by education, I can become quite cynical about the state of man at times.

Left to the devices of the media, one might be tempted to only see men of faith as corrupt, anti-intellectual, racist, homophobic, child molesting chauvinists. Mr. Gray Beard, on the other hand, showed the less visible, but still powerful side of faith—its role as a positive motivator toward charity and kindness in everyday life. Mr. Gray Beard was able to relate to my implied poverty because of his faith. Mr. Gray Beard, a man of faith, helped restore some of my faith in man.

Not all my experiences were deep matters of faith and insight—some were just surreal. This is the case when I think about my interaction with one of the female donors. To combat boredom at the exit ramp, one becomes a professional "people-watcher" out of necessity. Sometimes the sights that you truly see can be even stranger than fiction.

August 13 was my eighth day out panhandling, and it was a hot one. I had spent most of my morning standing around sweating in my boots. As you might recall, this happened to be the same day I received my lowest donation (four cents) and by mid-afternoon I assumed I had already found my noteworthy writing event for the day. Trying to keep my mind off the heat and the monotony, I began to daydream about everything cool, refreshing, or even mildly entertaining.

At 3:37 P.M. there was a flash of something distinctive coming down the ramp that woke me out of my stupor. A black and white Vespa scooter stood out from the normal blur of sedans and SUVs. I remember thinking, "Who rides a Vespa on the freeway, anyways?"

Driving the scooter was a willowy young woman in a black and white polka-dotted summer dress, a strange mirage emerging from the summer heat. I was probably staring noticeably when she looked my way and started to cut across the turn lanes. When she pointed her finger and gestured to the lot behind me, I actually did the stupid point at myself and shrug thing. There wasn't anyone else standing there, but for a moment, I couldn't fathom that she was really gesturing at *me*. She pointed again as she drove past, floated around the right hand turn, and glided into what I now thought of as *my* lot.

She was in the process of dismounting the scooter as I rounded the fence. I was momentarily struck with the impression that Audrey Hepburn had driven right out of an Italian movie set and into my parking lot. The only thing that would have made the moment more Hollywood would have been for the driver to shake out her hair in slow motion as she removed her helmet.

The slender female, now off the scooter, put down her kickstand and opened up the seat of the vehicle to dig out a petite purse from a small storage compartment. As she fished around in the purse, she said hello and mentioned she had also been to Iraq. That took me off guard. Being the dolt I am, I did not follow up with questions to find out more. This was partly out of self-defense—the more one talks about personal matters the thinner one's cover becomes—and partly because the awkwardness I felt in my role as a bum had suddenly, and exponentially, increased.

Instead of asking if she had been in the service, I settled on a much lamer comeback. "You have a nice scooter."

"Oh, thanks," she said and handed me a twenty dollar bill.

That was it. Ms. Hepburn started putting her purse away and picking up her helmet.

"Thanks for your kindness," I called as I started to walk back to my corner. Before I knew it, she had remounted her scooter and ridden off to her rendezvous with Gregory Peck.

Is there a point to remembering this episode, other than to admit that I have seen *Roman Holiday*? Yes, the woman in the polka dot dress serves as a good reminder that economics is the study of people—people that are diverse, individual, and unexpected.

I started this study with my own stereotypes about the people who would be my donors. I assumed I knew the type of people, both male and female, who give money to strangers. Before actually standing out there at the exit ramp, I would never have thought a young woman riding a scooter, dressed to the nines for a summer lawn party, would go out of her way to stop and give me twenty dollars. This study demolished some of my comfortable assumptions. It changed my understanding of charity and the people who give it. Ms. Hepburn happens to be just one example out of many. Sometimes charity looks a lot like a Hollywood movie.

# CHAPTER 5

---

# BAD NUMBERS

*"All economic statistics are best seen as a
peculiarly boring form of science fiction..."*

–PAUL KRUGMAN

Chronologically, we left off at the end of the third day, and
before exploring further topics, I want to bring you ahead
to the halfway mark of my study.

Day four is most notable for starting the slowest of any
day out at the exit ramp. For three whole hours I did not
receive a single data point to record. By 12:00 P.M. I was
beginning to seriously think it was possible to go a whole day
without a single donation. Panhandling is not exciting—and
when you don't receive any donations, it can actually be considered a form of mental torture.

During this time, however, I did receive a call from the
pastor of my local church. I had to hide behind a hedge to
take the call (so as to not blow my cover). Apparently, another
member of my church had driven past, seen me begging, and
become concerned. He talked to the pastor who, in turn,

called to see if I was in financial straits—which reminded me that, again, I really should have told more people about this study or picked a panhandling spot farther from home. I reassured my pastor I was not in need of alms—just data.

After this short hiatus, I went back to panhandling and bleakly began calculating what a full day without donations would do for my overall averages...when, suddenly, my luck changed. At 12:25 P.M. I received three dollars. The day was further salvaged by a series of high donations. Over the next several hours, I received two twenties, a fifteen dollar donation, a five spot, two more three dollar donations, and a single one dollar bill—a clean seventy dollars over seven hours. Day four was my third day in a row where I earned above minimum wage. I was beginning to get excited. It was beginning to look like panhandling might indeed be a relatively profitable endeavor.

Days five and six only added to the rosy outlook. On day five I earned a total of $88.26 over seven hours for an average hourly wage of $12.61. Day six was a sliver better at $79.00 over six hours for an average hourly wage of $13.17. With half my study done, I had completed five out of six days that earned more than—and sometimes considerably more than—minimum wage. The total cash earnings I had collected were $480.22. The study was not over, however—six more days remained.

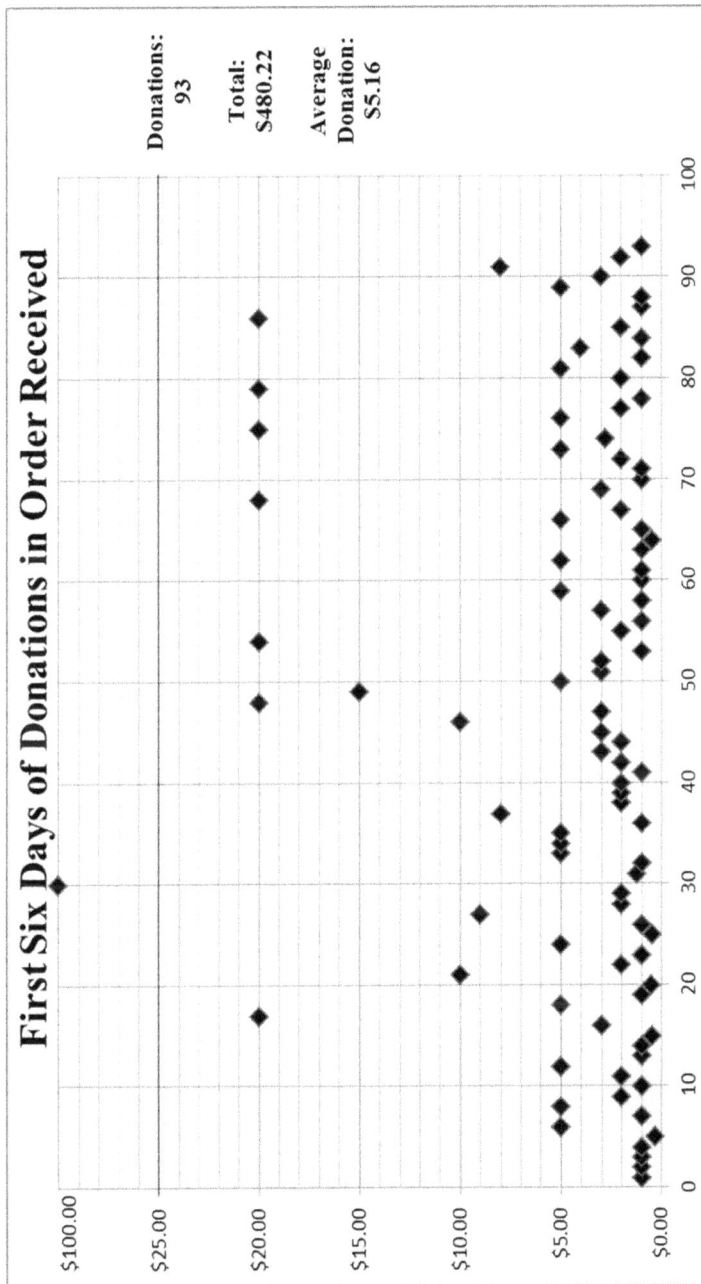

First Six Days of Donations in Order Received

Donations: 93

Total: $480.22

Average Donation: $5.16

*Figure 3: Days One through Six - Donations*

## Average Hourly Wage for First Six Days Panhandling

Day 1 — $5.13
Day 2 — $10.21
Day 3 — $24.63
Day 4 — $10.00
Day 5 — $12.61
Day 6 — $13.17

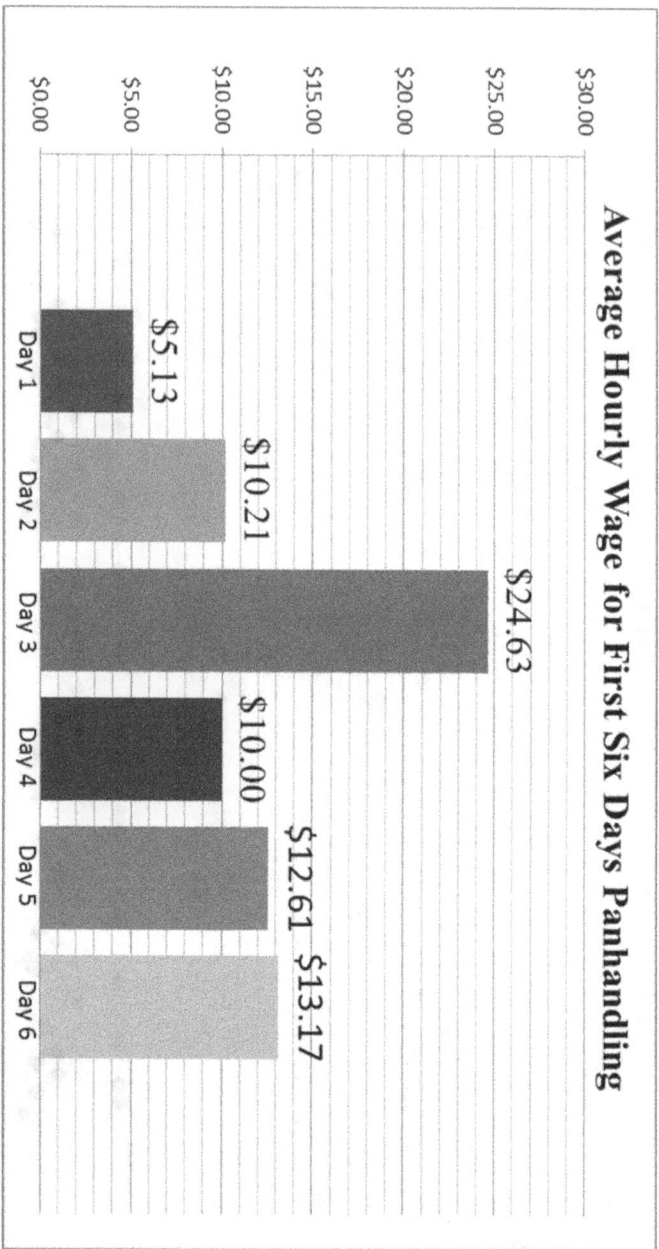

*Figure 4: Days One through Six - Averages*

This seems as good a place as any to make an abrupt transition to talking about the things that did *not* work in this study. This is the part you always leave out of college economic papers so you look smarter than you actually are. While I was highly encouraged by the results of the first half of my study, I was also beginning to realize that some of my attempts at collecting data were going to fail, and fail big. There is nothing like doing field work to teach one a little humility.

## SOCIOECONOMIC CARS

Hands down, the greatest failure of this study was my attempt to record the make and model of each vehicle belonging to the donors. My original goal was to record this information to use as a proxy for socioeconomic status. The reasoning went something like this: if I record and then price the car type of each donor, I can get a general feel for what economic class that donor comes from.

Simply, and maybe overly simplistically, if the donor drove a nice new Land Rover or BMW, I could speculate he was upper middle class; if a 1990 Honda Accord, maybe blue collar and lower class. While not a perfect proxy for socioeconomic status, the car data might prove useful and open up a new dimension to the study.

There was one very big and ultimately fatal flaw in my attempt at recording such data—I am not a car guy. Growing up, I was an aviation kid; I could (and probably still can) identify every American wartime plane from WWI to the Gulf War. I know bubkis about the make and models of cars.

This general lack of interest in cars became a problem that

was compounded by the fact that most transactions at the exit ramp lasted only the few seconds it took for someone to hand cash out of a window. As I stood at the corner trying to identify cars, I was completely and utterly out of my league. I am sure some people can record a car's make, model, and year after a single glance. I am not one of those people.

The compromise I came up with on the spot was not inspired. I ended up recording the *style* of each vehicle, jotting down car, SUV, pickup truck, or van in place of make, model, and year. If you know how to make economic sense of the fact that 67 of the donations came from cars, 47 from SUV's, 39 from pickup trucks, 20 from vans, 2 from semi-trucks, and 1 from a scooter, you are probably a better economist than I.

I, however, think it best to chalk up the recording of socio-economic status, by proxy of vehicle, as a well-intentioned but complete and utter failure. Damn.

## WHAT'S YOUR AGE, AGAIN?

The second data-gathering issue I faced was not as much a debacle as the first. In regards to collecting the age of donors, recording the correct data proved difficult, but maybe not to such a critical degree as my first example.

One of the downsides of collecting data undercover is that you cannot actually survey your donors to find accurate statistical information. I attempted to collect the age of each donor by the only means available—a guesstimate. Or to phrase it more technically, I used the S.W.A.G. method—a "scientific wild-ass guess."

Although a person's age can be deceiving and I was

recording my data solely on visual impressions, I like to think that I am a fairly astute observer of the differences between teenagers, middle-agers, and octogenarians. Guessing an approximate age is a bit more forgiving than guessing a make, model, and year on a car.

To deal with the inherent inaccuracy of guessing people's ages by sight, I broke down age into categories. I used three categories: young, middle-aged, and old. For the young, I counted anyone who appeared to be under 25. For the middle-aged, I grouped people looking to be 25-49. For the old, I noted down anyone 50 or over.

On the assumption that I am relatively accurate at guessing a person's age, this is what I found. Of the 185 recorded donations, 20 were from young donors, 148 were from middle-aged donors, and 17 were from old donors. Percentage-wise, that is 11% from young donors, 80% from middle-aged, and 9% from old.

What does this tell us? Nothing, by itself. But returning to the 2010 U.S. Census data, we can compare the numbers against the greater population.[4] According to the Census, 15-24 year olds make up 12.2% of Clackamas County. Ages 25-49 account for 32.3% and ages 50-79 make up interestingly also 32.3% of the population. The remaining 23.2% of the population comes in either older or younger.

Again we can narrow this broad population into drivers. Looking into Oregon's Department of Motor Vehicles

---

4  United States Census Bureau, "Profile of General Population and Housing Characteristics: 2010," American Fact Finder, U.S. Department of Commerce, http://factfinder2.census.gov/faces/tableservices/jsf/pages/productview.xhtml?pid=DEC_10_DP_DPDP1 (accessed 6 July 2013).

statistics we can find *Drivers of Issuance by Age.*[5] According to this list, ages 14-24 make up 12.5% of Oregon drivers, ages 25-49 make up 44.1%, and ages 50-79 make up 39.3%.

It is hard to know what to make of these numbers. Both by the population of Clackamas County and by Oregon insured driver ages, the youth donated in accordance with their statistical percentages. This is not true, however, of our other two categories. The middle-aged made up 80% of my donors, but interestingly, they only make up 44.1% of drivers. Conversely, the elderly made up only 9% of my donors, although they account for 39.3% of insured drivers.

This leads to the obvious question: *What explains the low donation percentage of older drivers and the high percentage of middle-aged?* Here we get into the realm of pure hypothesis—answers that seem plausible but have not been proven one way or the other.

It *might* have something to do with incomes. A lot of people ages 25-49 are in their prime wage earning years, while at the same time many retirees face the problems of a fixed income. Maybe the discrepancy is as simple as the fact that middle-aged drivers have the most means to be charitable and therefore are the most charitable.

To make another guess at it, we could also look into the hours spent behind the wheel by each age group. Do elderly drivers drive as much as middle-aged drivers? Maybe it is a driving frequency issue, with the elderly on the road less often and with less opportunity to donate.

To take another shot in the dark, we could examine the

---

5   Oregon DMV, "Drivers of Issuance by Age," 12/31/2011, Oregon. gov, http://www.oregon.gov/ODOT/DMV/docs/stats/doi_age/2011_ doi_by_age.pdf (accessed 6 July 2013).

issue of generational mores. Maybe my parents' generation and the generations before were raised with a different mentality towards begging. I will not pretend to be a sociologist or anthropologist, but the data seems to raise these kinds of questions. With the inexact method I utilized to guess the age of donors, this data has clearly earned a place in this chapter of failed experimentation. However, the discrepancy between the numbers I recorded and the numbers the Census records of the general population, does raise some intriguing questions. In the end, the data is interesting but it leaves us guessing.

## THE PERCENTAGE OF DRIVERS WHO GIVE TO PANHANDLERS…I THINK…MAYBE?

The third failure of this study was not a failure due to guesswork. I was able to record proper data this time—I just don't trust it. This failure came as I attempted to determine what percentage of drivers donate to panhandlers.

Sounds simple right? I only needed two numbers: the number of people who traveled past my sign and the number of people who gave. Unfortunately, this turned out to be more complicated than it appeared.

The second number, of course, is easy; I collected it just by recording each transaction at the exit ramp. The first number is the rub. How many people *did* pass by my sign? I created a strategy to find out, but the more I thought back on it, the more I became uncomfortable with my method. Below I will explain how I attempted to find out the overall number of cars that could have donated. Does my method work? You be the judge.

Needing to get a count of the cars that went through my intersection, I bought a simple click counter like the ones baseball umpires use to count strikes. Hiding my hand in my pocket, I counted cars with the click of a button. *Click!* One. *Click!* Two. *Click!* Three. I started this on the second day of the study and counted 758 vehicles.

The main problem with this number was that it was actually quite subjective. At first, I was overly concerned that I collect only the number of people who had a legitimate chance to donate. This means, in practice, that I counted only the cars that I thought were in a *position* to donate—not all the cars that passed by.

Initially, I did not believe a vehicle ten cars back from where I stood at the exit ramp had a legitimate chance of donating. I also did not count the cars that passed by on a green light for the same reason. Generally, this means I counted the closest six to eight stopped cars. These are the ones I considered to be potential donors.

As the donations started to come in, however, I realized just how flawed this methodology was. Drivers who may have been farther back in the line of stopped cars went around the turn and used the lot behind me to stop and donate. More than one car made a quick cash donation during a green light. A couple donations even came from people throwing crumpled up cash out a window as they drove by. These cars were not captured in my limited counting method, but they still donated—hence, my discomfort with the strategy I used to figure out how many cars could have donated, a strategy I devised before I went out into the field and learned the dynamics.

I will share my numbers as they are, but I would not bet anything more than a piece of cold pizza on their accuracy. In sequential order starting on the second day, and ending on the eleventh, here is the vehicle count as I recorded it: 758, 925, 1053, 833, 1024, 1150, 866, 684, 1054, and 1177. (Keep in mind these numbers were recorded over different amounts of time spent at the exit ramp: 4.5, 6.75, 7, 7, 6, 6.75, 7, 7, 7, and 8.5 hours respectively). The number of donations for the same days were: 10, 20, 8, 22, 17, 13, 16, 17, 17 and 16.

With that, the percentage of people who donated—out of all those who had the opportunity to do so (using my admittedly flawed numbers)—comes to: 1.3%, 2.2%, 0.8%, 2.5%, 1.7%, 1.1%, 1.8%, 2.5%, 1.6%, and 1.4%. This averages out to 1.7% of drivers donating money, one out of every 59 drivers.

If anything, these percentages are high as I most likely did not count enough cars. While I can't really use these numbers in good faith to draw any conclusions, I do think they inconclusively reinforce at least one statement I have already made: panhandling really is very, very boring. You watch a lot of cars go by.

Unhappy with my failed methodology, I made a second attempt to get the population size of possible donors at my exit ramp. I turned to Oregon's Department of Transportation and their traffic volume reports in search of better numbers. On ODOT's website under *Ramp Interchange Volume Diagrams*, I found the 2011 Annual Average Daily Traffic number for my exact spot—12,870.[6]

---

6 Oregon Department of Transportation, "Ramp Interchange Volume Diagrams: 2011 Annual Average Daily Traffic," Oregon.gov, http://www.oregon.gov/ODOT/TD/TDATA/tsm/docs/Ramps_2011.pdf (accessed 6 July 2013).

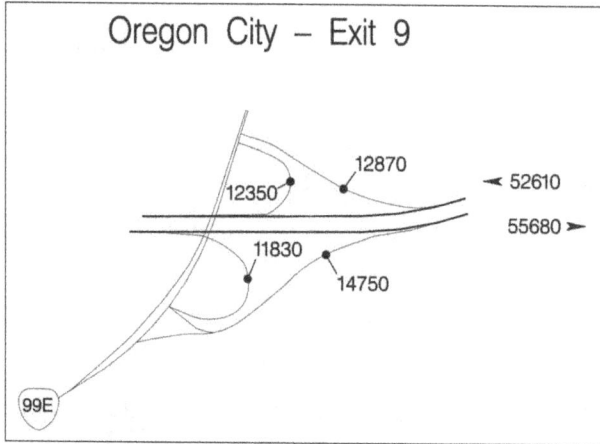

**Oregon City – Exit 9**

12870

12350

52610

55680

11830

14750

99E

*Figure 5: AADT Numbers for Oregon City - Exit 9*

For those not up on their transportation lingo, the Annual Average Daily Traffic number is a measurement of traffic flow. It is created by taking the yearly amount of traffic over any one spot and dividing it by 365. Basically, this means we can say 12,870 cars use my exit ramp on an "average" day.

One interesting thing about finding the AADT numbers is that it allowed me to compare the traffic flow at my exit with the traffic flow of other popular panhandling locations along Interstate 205. Initially, I had assumed that my exit, being farther from the Portland metro center than others, would be less traveled. The AADT numbers, however, showed that the traffic flow at my location was fairly similar to that of most of the exits along the interstate. Only a few exits were recorded to have significantly higher traffic flows, and—hypothetically—better panhandling spots.

The 12,870 vehicles that pass my spot daily do so in a twenty-four hour period. Since I did not attempt any Le Mans style panhandling, we need to divide the AADT number for a twenty-four hour period into the hours I actually was at my post. That gives us a traffic flow of 2413 vehicles (instead of the 758 I recorded on the second day). The rest of the days' counts using the AADT number adjusted for the hours I spent at the exit ramp are: 3620, 3754, 3754, 3218, 3620, 3754, 3754, 3754, and finally 4558.

Still with me? Let's use these numbers like we did above to get the percentage of drivers who gave monetary donations. Here it is: on day two of the overall study—the first day I collected my own vehicle flow numbers—0.41% of drivers donated according to the ODOT numbers. The rest of the days follow at 0.55%, 0.21%, 0.59%, 0.53%, 0.36%, 0.43%, 0.45%, 0.45%, and 0.35% respectively. The average for the complete ten days tells us that 0.43% of drivers donated—or, to put it another way, one out of every 233 drivers.

I feel more confident using ODOT's numbers to make conclusions, but they are not without their own set of problems. For one, the Annual Average Daily Traffic number is not seasonally adjusted. I conducted my study in the middle of summer, and I have to think more people drive in the good weather than the bad. The AADT numbers also do not account for different traffic flow during different times of day. How many of the 12,870 vehicles traveled at night when I was not recording donations? Probably far fewer than traveled during the day—which would mean even more drivers passed by me than my calculations state. Even the official numbers for average traffic flow can only help so much.

I have played with the numbers, trying to get a picture of how many drivers *were* monetarily charitable out of how many drivers *could have been* charitable. I may have gotten the numbers into the right ballpark, but it is a really big ball-park. This avenue of investigation was not an utter failure—as was my experiment to record socioeconomic status—but the subjectivity on the one end and the guesswork on the other present a real challenge to accuracy.

## I AM NOT A RACIST

Fortunately, not all my attempts at recording data had the problems of the last three examples. Despite the incongruity of including this in the chapter of failed numbers, one data-capturing success was recording the race of each donor. This required neither the guesswork nor the subjectivity of the previous categories of data compilation. The results are, thankfully, uncontroversial but fascinating.

Of the 185 donations where I recorded the race of the donor, 169 were from White donors, 3 from Blacks, 6 from Asians, 5 from Hispanics, and 2 from Pacific Islanders. Changed to percentages, 91.35% of my donations came from Whites, 1.62% from Blacks, 3.24% from Asians, 2.70% from Hispanics, and 1.08% from Pacific Islanders.

Now, before any white supremacist starts singing the great praises of Aryan generosity, these numbers need context. Looking at the U.S. Census Bureau's 2011 State and County QuickFacts webpage, we can get the demographics for Clack-amas County. According to the most recent Census, Whites make up 91.1% of the population (with approximately 7% of that number being those of Hispanic descent who identify themselves as White). Blacks make up 1% of the population, Asians 3.8%, and Pacific Islanders 0.3%. The remaining 3.8%

of the population consists of American Indians and people who identify themselves as belonging to two (unspecified) races.

The similarity of the numbers is telling. From all appearances, my experience at the exit ramp of receiving money from White donors 169 times out of 185 is close to what should be expected according to the greater population demographics. There is some play in the numbers as the percentages don't correspond exactly, but they are, relatively speaking, pretty darn close.

Keep in mind the small sample size of this study. When I received my second donation from a Pacific Islander, the percentage changed from 0.54% to 1.08%.

If we don't split hairs, it is safe to say that each race donated in close proportion to their population percentage in Clackamas County. As with the gender numbers, the results of looking into race and charity in this study are not polemic. I would be highly uncomfortable with anyone using my small sample to draw any grand conclusion about a race's charity or lack thereof. That is a very different area of research and light years beyond the scope of this aspiring economist's modest goals.

Investigating the peripheral data I collected has been an interesting side note to this study but it is not our true objective. Some of the data, like that on gender and race, provided sound results and thought-provoking information about charity. Some of the data, like that of age and vehicle description, failed to product anything usable at all. Other data, like the vehicle counts, fell somewhere in-between, bogged down in ambiguity due to flawed methodology. Fortunately, the most important data does not rely on guesswork. It is now time to look at the data I set out to collect in the first place—the money.

# CHAPTER 6

# THE PROFITABILITY OF PANHANDLING

*"Political Economy or Economics is a study of mankind
in the ordinary business of life; it examines that
part of individual and social action which is most
closely connected with the attainment and with
the use of the material requisites of wellbeing."*

–ALFRED MARSHALL

*How well does panhandling work?* Or to put it another way:
*What can a transient make per hour?* It is the question
that started this all. It is the question I set out to answer with
firsthand experience. Each day that I stood at the exit ramp
under the pretense of being impoverished, I progressed closer
to the answer—one donation at a time.

Learning the demographics of donors was an informative
side result of pursuing my original question. Discovering that
the generosity of people went far beyond simple cash was also
an unexpected benefit. But as interesting as all this is, I suspect it is *not* why you picked up the book. I am guessing that
you—like me—want to know how much money a cardboard
sign and a well-placed freeway exit can earn a person. I think

I have beaten around the bush long enough; let's settle this. It is time to answer the one question I set out to answer.

Day seven through twelve continued in the general pattern of the first six days. Each day was unique, but none were particularly remarkable. Many of the stories that happened on those days I have already shared with you. Instead of continuing to go donation by donation and rehashing the same narrative, it will be more profitable to change tack and look at this study as a whole.

Here are my daily cash earnings in order, the amount of total cash I brought home each day:

| Daily Cash Earnings | |
|---|---|
| Day 1 | $30.76 |
| Day 2 | $45.95 |
| Day 3 | $166.25 |
| Day 4 | $70.00 |
| Day 5 | $88.26 |
| Day 6 | $79.00 |
| Day 7 | $41.85 |
| Day 8 | $93.05 |
| Day 9 | $87.75 |
| Day 10 | $87.35 |
| Day 11 | $44.45 |
| Day 12 | $53.30 |

To save you the trouble of reaching for your calculator, the total cash I took home over the twelve days of panhandling comes out to a very respectable $887.97.

This number alone should give you some indication of

what is coming. To turn the total cash into an hourly wage is our next step. The average hourly wage for each day is:

| Average Hourly Wage | |
| --- | --- |
| Day 1 | $5.13 |
| Day 2 | $10.21 |
| Day 3 | $24.63 |
| Day 4 | $10.00 |
| Day 5 | $12.61 |
| Day 6 | $13.17 |
| Day 7 | $6.20 |
| Day 8 | $13.29 |
| Day 9 | $12.54 |
| Day 10 | $12.48 |
| Day 11 | $5.23 |
| Day 12 | $8.20 |

If you have an old pay stub ready, now is the time to look at it. The next number is the average hourly wage I collected for two weeks of panhandling. From the start, the premise of this experiment was to treat panhandling like a job and compare it against a real job paying at least minimum wage. *Can a panhandler earn more than minimum wage?* The answer, from my 80 hours of experience, is a resounding *yes!* At the end of my twelve days, I had earned an average of $11.10 an hour.

Not only is this comfortably above minimum wage, I actually earned more money panhandling than I did the previous summer working mall security for ten dollars an hour. That's something to think about.

(If you are one of the readers who decided earlier to discount the hundred dollar bill as an outlier, this drops the average hourly wage to $9.85—somewhat less impressive, but still over minimum wage.)

This is not even taking into account taxes. Using a generic gross-up payroll calculator, readily available with a Google search, I calculated that in order to net $887.97 after state and federal taxes, I would have had to gross $1083.75. Or, in other words, I would actually have had to work a job that paid $13.55 an hour to match the profitability of my panhandling enterprise. By this accounting, begging is not a bad job—at least, if money is the only consideration.

Now that we are looking at the complete study we can also look at some of the standard statistical interpretations of the data. The average donation, taking all 187 donations into account, came in at $4.75. The median amount, or the value that is in the middle of the data when it is arranged in ascending order smallest value to largest, was $2.00. The mode, or the value that occurs the greatest number of times, was, as you may have intuitively guessed, $1.00.

I will get to the implications of my results in good time, but first I want to manipulate the numbers some more. One of the questions I had, along with my general curiosity about overall earnings, was about *which hour of the day* would prove the most profitable. I treated my panhandling as a quasi-job, and I worked (loosely) nine to five. Does the data show that I could have increased or decreased my earnings by selectively panhandling during peak traffic times? To find answers, let's look for the most profitable hour.

Here my irregular schedule plays some havoc with the numbers. The nine to ten o'clock hour is basically unusable because of different start times. Some days I started at 9:15 A.M. and other days at nine sharp. Because I did not work

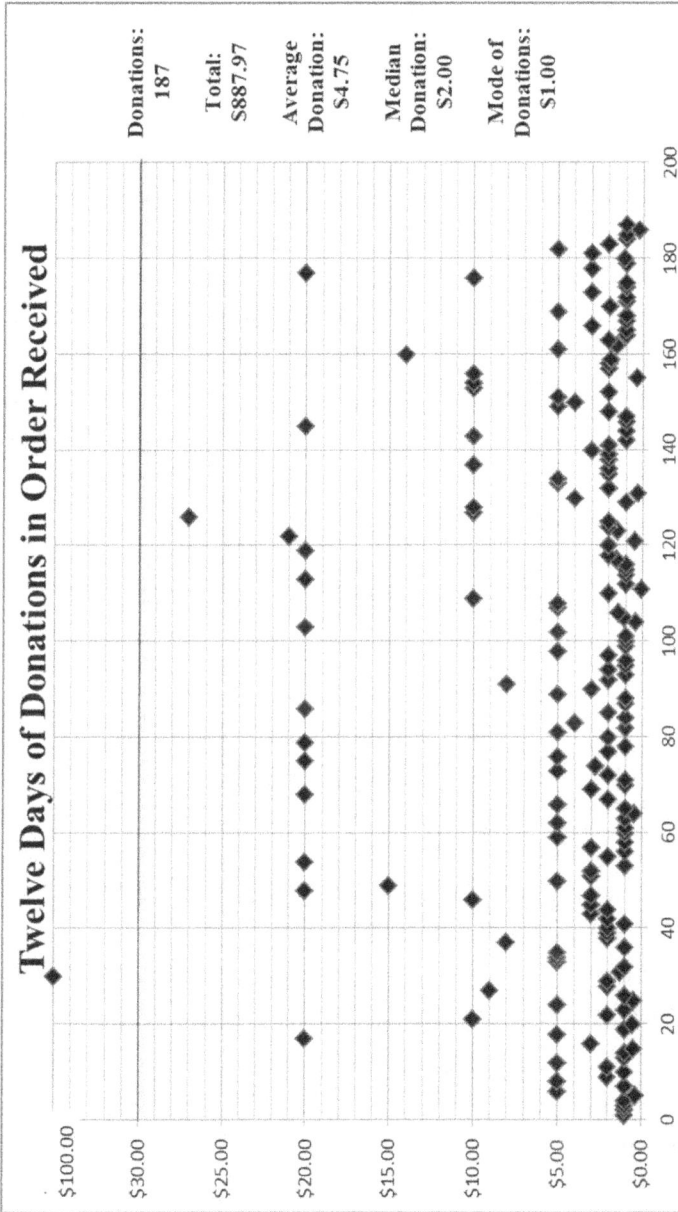

*Figure 6: Complete Study - Donations*

this full hour each day, I can't compare the nine o'clock hour against the rest. The ten o'clock, eleven o'clock, and twelve o'clock hours are all fair game, as I worked the full hour each and every day of this study. The one o'clock and two o'clock hours were each bisected by my lunch break from 1:30 to 2:30 P.M. The afternoon hours of three to four and four to five are complete—except for the fact that I panhandled only 10 afternoons, losing my spot to the female panhandler on the second day and finishing my eighty hours early on the last day. With these caveats, the numbers still tell a story.

The most profitable hour, using a weighted average for hours actually worked, was the eleven o'clock hour. Using my considerable pop-psychology skills, I at first attributed this to people being the happiest when going to lunch—and, therefore, the most generous. It sounds good, right?

An interesting thing happens, however, if you discount the single hundred dollar bill I received during the eleven o'clock hour. Without that single donation, the hour falls from the *most* profitable to the *second least* profitable. So much for happy lunch-goers donating more...and so much for my pop-psychology skills. The eleven o'clock hour was only the most profitable hour thanks to one donor.

The second most profitable hour—or the first, if we discount the outlier donation—was the four o'clock hour, the start of the evening rush hour. The third most profitable hour, if you add the two halves together was the 1:00-1:30 and the 2:30-3:00 hour. Now that I have actual data, I know that choosing my lunch break for the time I did might have been a mistake...apparently, the 1:30-2:30 hour could have been prime panhandling time.

After that, continuing in order from most to least profitable comes the twelve o'clock hour, the ten o'clock hour, and then the three o'clock hour.

Even with the caveats and adjusting for the irregular schedule I worked, a pattern does emerge. I am not sure you need an aspiring economist to tell you this, but the most profitable hours at the exit ramp generally corresponded with peak traffic times. Panhandling during the lunch and evening rush hours paid more than panhandling during the early morning and middle afternoon hours.

If I ever return to this type of field work, it would be interesting to find numbers for the later evening and earlier morning rush hours. I did "stay late at work" on two days and record donations from five to six, but it would be foolish to make conclusions from only two data samples. However, from what I did record, there is a case to be made that if I had been more selective with my panhandling times I could have increased my hourly wage.

If I dropped the least profitable hours and worked later into the evening rush, my results *might* have turned out even better. It's hard to say. Along those lines, you will notice I never did work any of the early morning rush hours. In my defense, it was my summer break, and I have never really been a morning person. Hence, the profits of being an early riser remain an open question.

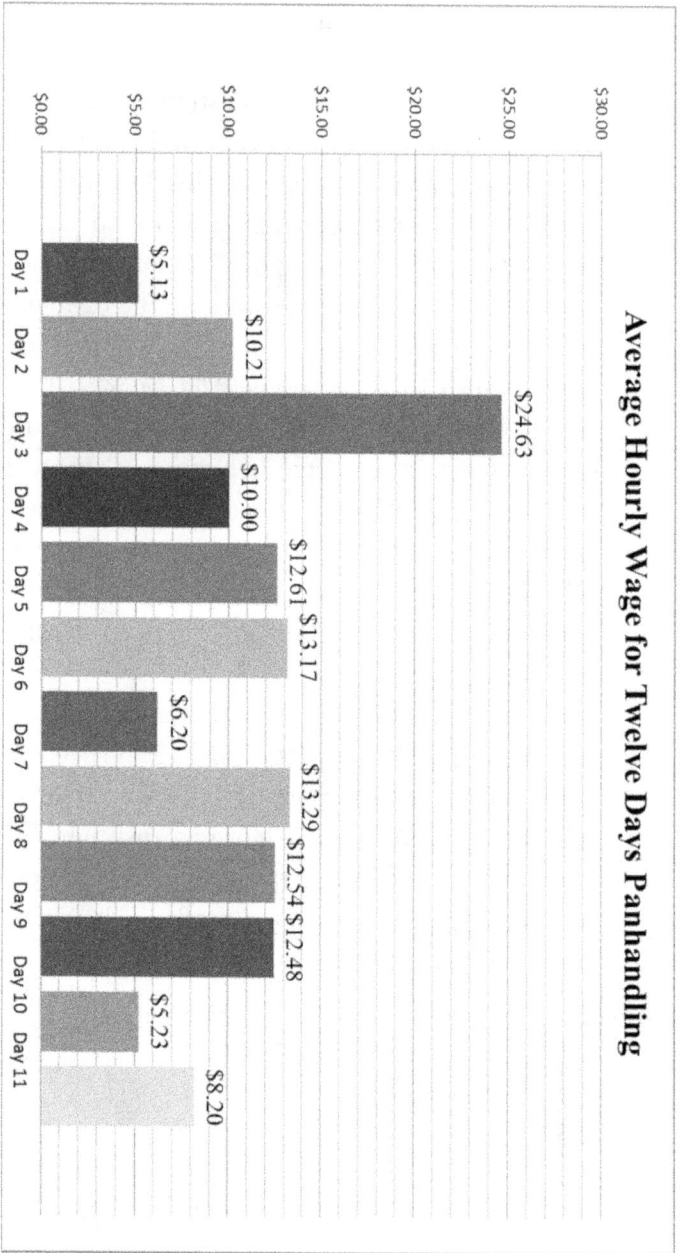

Average Hourly Wage for Twelve Days Panhandling

Day 1: $5.13
Day 2: $10.21
Day 3: $24.63
Day 4: $10.00
Day 5: $12.61
Day 6: $13.17
Day 7: $6.20
Day 8: $13.29
Day 9: $12.54
Day 10: $12.48
Day 11: $5.23
$8.20

*Figure 7: Complete Study - Averages*

# CHAPTER 7

---

# IMPLICATIONS

*"It may sound noble to say, 'Damn economics, let us build up a decent world'—but it is, in fact, merely irresponsible."*

–F. A. HAYEK

I earned $11.10 an hour while standing at the exit ramp panhandling. What does one make of this? It is one thing to record the data—it is another thing to interpret it. I first fell in love with economics by the way of political theory—not by way of mathematics. Numbers are only interesting to me when they provide information about the way people make choices. Economics is not physics. It is only a worthwhile academic pursuit if we are courageous enough to place a value on the numbers.

I suspect there will be two general reactions to this study. Those with a preconceived notion of panhandlers as scam artists might use the high wage I earned to reinforce their beliefs. Panhandlers are not in real need—just look at how much money they can make!

On the other hand, people with different preconceptions

might be highly encouraged by my results. They might say that my success proves that every donor's dollar (or twenty dollars) actually makes a real difference in someone's life. Every penny adds up and helps pave a path out of poverty.

Readers will look either positively or negatively on the fact that I earned $11.10 an hour. Each view probably has more to do with a reader's political and philosophical leanings than with what this study actually reveals.

Think about the negative view often put forth that panhandlers are scam artists. We've all heard the story about the panhandler dropping his sign, rounding the corner, and climbing into his Mercedes-Benz. Does my study prove this to be the norm? No, not exactly.

From the start, I never intended to go to the exit ramp to figure out who was in real need and who was not—to expose who panhandles because of real poverty and who panhandles because it pays. I can't speak to whether any particular individual panhandling at any particular exit ramp is or is not involved in a money racket. Knowing someone *can* make $11.10 per hour does not reveal which person *needs* to make $11.10 per hour. That is a different study for a different time and a different book.

Does this mean the data I collected is mute on the subject? Not necessarily. What I can say from my experience and my data is this: there is definitely an *incentive* to panhandle beyond doing it for subsistence level living. The ability to make a competitive wage will, according to economic theory, bring in people to panhandle, taking advantage of the high wage opportunity. While I can't say who is panhandling out of real need and who is panhandling because it pays well, I can say this: panhandling pays well enough for people to take advantage of it.

You don't need a supply and demand graph or complex formulas to grasp this. Just take me, for example. After earning what I did at the exit ramp, economically speaking, I should have continued panhandling all summer. I earned more money panhandling than I did working my last summer job. Even though I could not be considered poor or homeless, I would have irrefutably benefited monetarily from continuing to panhandle.

It is understandable to take a negative view of panhandling, to think that all panhandlers are "working the system," when the system is so obviously something that *can* be worked. What about a more positive view of generosity toward panhandlers? What about the idea that each donation matters because it could be the one act of kindness that changes a person's life? While in one sense this view is also understandable, I think this study's results call into question the effects of such generosity. Poverty is a more complex problem than can be solved by giving a dollar to a beggar and driving away.

Although this might be the most controversial thing I say in this book, I believe that panhandling is not ultimately a result of income poverty—that is, a lack of income cannot be the root cause of panhandling, at least not in any long term sense. This is true because panhandling itself, as I discovered, provides an income that can lift one out of poverty. In a perfect world, the need to panhandle would be a self-correcting problem.

Don't take my word for it—do the math. If you will allow me the small assumption of doubling my two week earnings to represent a monthly budget, then our hypothetical panhandler has a monthly income of $1,775.94. Let's see how far that gets him.

First, we need to find our transient somewhere to live. A simple ten minute search on Craigslist finds an Oregon City apartment for $595 a month. It's not the cheapest apartment, but it's on the low end. I have never lived in an apartment by myself, so there is no need to assume our transient can't also share the cost with friends. Split with a roommate, the lodging would only cost $297.50 a month. (I earned that amount in the first four days of panhandling.) If our transient is even a little bit popular, he could split the cost with two roommates, further dropping housing costs to $198.33.

But let's be conservative about the number of people willing to live with our panhandler. Assuming only a two-way split on the rent, we find our no-longer-homeless panhandler still has $1,478.44 to get by on for the month.

After shelter, the very next thing I always think about is food—a man has to eat. For some food budget numbers, we can turn to United States Department of Agriculture's Center for Nutrition Policy and Promotion.

According to the *Official USDA Food Plans: Cost of Food at Home at Four Levels, U.S. Average, July 2012*, a 19-50 year old male's monthly average food cost can be separated into four plans. The thrifty plan comes in at $217.56 a month, the low-cost plan at $281.04, the moderate plan at $350.76, and finally the liberal plan tops out at $431.64 a month.[7] You can

7    Center for Nutrition Policy and Promotion, "Official USDA Food Plans: Cost of Food at Home at Four Levels, U.S. Average, July 2012," U.S. Department of Agriculture, http://www.cnpp.usda.gov/Publications/FoodPlans/2012/CostofFoodJul2012.pdf (accessed 6 July 2013).

play with the numbers as you like, but I am going to assume our hypothetical panhandler has some self-discipline and lives on the low-cost plan. It should also be noted that his purchased food will be supplemented by the food gifted to him at the exit ramp—a not insignificant quantity of McDonald's. After food, our panhandler still has $1,197.40 to spend.

Now there are a lot of little expenses to life that we don't need to explore in exhaustive detail. You know how to balance a budget as well as I do (probably better, if you ask my wife). There is, however, one more expense I want to insert into our panhandler's budget. My contention is that panhandling pays well enough to lift someone out of poverty. This implies some sort of change in the employability of the panhandler. We can price this too.

In Oregon City, the location of this study, the easiest way to improve one's vocational skills is at Clackamas Community College. The college boasts over 80 career technical programs.[8] Let's choose one—welding technology—to gain some insight into the cost of acquiring a new skill set to boost employability.

To earn a welding certificate, one needs 53-56 credits which can be completed in an estimated 33 weeks—three college quarters. The current cost of tuition for these credits is $6,504.50-6,755.00 plus another $1,178.00 in books. Let's estimate $7807 total for tuition and books.

Three college quarters, the time needed to earn the welding technology certificate, span roughly nine months. If we divide the cost over those months, our panhandler needs

---

8  Clackamas Community College, "CCC Career Technical Programs," Clackamas Community College, http://www.clackamas.edu/Career_Technical_Programs.aspx (accessed 6 July 2013).

to pay $867.44 a month. Even a sum like this will not break the budget. With housing, food, and now school paid for, our reforming panhandler is left with $329.96 a month in disposable income, enough to still buy his smokes.

I know this exercise has been built on a lot of assumptions. I am assuming a panhandler can earn a steady income for nine months or more. My data set is awfully small to make such a big leap. I am also assuming that he will be able to fit his full time panhandling schedule in around his full time school schedule (although this might be the least of my assumptions since I worked a full time job while taking a full load of classes at community college).

But while I have made some assumptions, I have also estimated high for many of the costs. I did not account for financial aid such as Pell Grants. I did not account for the savings a person committed to austerity could find when properly motivated to carry out this plan.

A lot of variables, more than our simple example accounted for, go into a panhandling budget—not all of them clear. Regardless, the *possibility* of earning a way out of poverty through panhandling appears eminently feasible.

Even if you find fault with my panhandler's imaginary budget and proposed course of education, the fact remains that a panhandler who earns $887.97 in two weeks is not impoverished. The United States poverty line in 2012 for a single individual under 65 is an annual income of $11,945.[9] Dividing that annual income into a two-week period gives us

---

9  United States Census Bureau, "Poverty Thresholds by Size of Family and Number of Children," U.S. Department of Commerce, http://www.census.gov/hhes/www/poverty/data/threshld/ (accessed 6 July 2013).

the figure $459.42. I made nearly twice that much. Extrapolating off my earnings and assuming they could remain constant over a year's time, we see that my annual income would have been $23,087.22—shockingly close to what I made when I was deployed in Iraq for a year.

In a way, this actually reinforces the positive view of donating to panhandlers, and I am sympathetic to it. Giving a dollar does appear to have the power to do some real good.

The problem is ultimately not found in the dollar but in the donor and the transient. In a perfect world, an impoverished and unemployed person would only need to panhandle to replace lost income until such time as he could find a replacement income. That might very well look like nine months of welding school. I suspect this is not the motivation of most panhandlers.

A donor could feel good about his contribution to a panhandler if he knew his donation—along with the donations of others—was actually being used to relieve and roll back the panhandler's poverty. The trouble is: donors can't know this.

Without building a relationship with the recipient of their charity, donors cannot know if their charity is actually charity at all. What evidence do you have that your one, five, or twenty actually changed anything for the transient?

I am not a critic of monetary generosity—don't misunderstand me. I am a critic of money *only* generosity. Taking sixty seconds out of our daily commute to give a dollar to a total stranger is nothing more than the economic equivalent of a drive by shooting—not exactly a strategy to win the "war on poverty." If we want our charity to matter, maybe we should take the time to aim.

At the exit ramp I was both surprised by people's eagerness

to be generous and dismayed by the inefficiency of so much of the generosity. I was surprised by how often people gave and by how much they gave—I was also disheartened by how often it amounted to nothing more than an exchange of money from one random individual to another random individual.

There were the bright exceptions where people offered both monetary relief and social help. The very first day I was offered a legitimate chance at a job. I was also offered a free ride to the V.A. Giving someone a twenty may be real generosity, but it is not on the same level as the generosity of actually offering someone help.

If someone wants to claim that giving money to a transient matters, then it needs to be offered in the same way that a father and son gave me both a ten dollar bill and a helping hand up. There must be more to the exchange than just an exchange of currency.

This is my interpretation of the data. Panhandling is not an economics problem first and foremost—and neither is the cure. The problem of panhandling must be seen as the result of social and personal factors—not financial. This understanding should be used to influence our policy, both personal and institutional, in regards to combating poverty.

Urban poverty might best be thought of as a modern day hydra—when we attempt to kill it with the golden sword of money, our act—however heroic—is doomed to fail. We need complex solutions to complex problems. Seeing a panhandler as someone who only needs money is putting the proverbial cart before the horse.

Ultimately, I will leave you, my readers, to find your own implications in and draw your own conclusions from my results. I have already accomplished my one true goal for this study—I found, quantitatively, the profitability of panhandling. That's good enough for one summer break. You are free to discount my work as that of an amateur, or you can see it as I do—as the first question in a much deeper conversation about modern urban poverty.

# EPILOGUE

*"A man must always live by his work, and his wages*
*must at least be sufficient to maintain him."*

–ADAM SMITH

So you are probably wondering what I did with the $887.97 I raked in at the exit ramp. Before I call it a day, I should probably tell you. Despite my wife making a compelling case for keeping it to pay for our son's medical bills, I decided to donate it to different veterans' charities. The money had been given—at least in part—in the spirit of helping a veteran, and I made sure each dollar went to real veterans that needed help. I did not use my veteran status in this study flippantly.

This might sound ironic, given that I criticized exclusively monetary charity in the previous chapter. The difference is in how I donated the money. Instead of giving the money randomly to strangers, I donated it to well-established organizations that would use it to build the types of relationships I could not.

Now that my study is finished, there is also the interesting question of where to go from here. Knowing what a panhandler can potentially make per hour has, in my mind, raised more questions than it has answered. This topic has significant room for further research, both on the same scale and at a much larger one. For some of the future questions I would like to answer, two weeks is really not enough time to collect data.

On the micro-level, I am still intrigued to find out: *Do humorous or serious signs work better? Do women or men panhandlers make more money? What happens to income if you add a three-legged dog to the equation? Can you exhaust a location by over-panhandling and becoming too familiar to the regulars on the ramp? Can you earn more at a suburban exit or a downtown one?* There are so many unanswered questions—so much more data to collect.

On the macro-level, I would like to research what happens when we stop looking at panhandling from the individual's perspective and start investigating it as a market. Using Portland's unique, regional, multi-county area known as Metro, an economist has the perfect metropolitan area for conducting this research.

The Metro boundary encompasses 463.3 square miles or 296,503.3 acres.[10] Portland, the biggest city in the Metro region, has a population of 593,820, and the Metro region has an estimated population of 1,556,300 persons.[11] How many of them participated in panhandling last year?

Taking a step further, how much money is exchanged in panhandling on a regional scale? What is the total market value of the panhandling industry? Now we are getting to something you can sink your intellectual teeth into.

---

10 Metro RLIS, "Area Measurements for the Metro Region, Counties and Cities," September 2010, Oregon Metro, http://library.oregon-metro.gov/files/AreaMeasurementsRegionCountyCity.pdf (accessed 6 July 2013).

11 Oregon Metro, "Population Inside Metro and UGB 1980 – present," U.S. Census and Metro Research Center, Oregon Metro, http://library.oregonmetro.gov/files/MetroUGBpop1980toPresent.pdf (accessed 6 July 2013).

Now admittedly, there may already be answers to some of these questions. Economics has a long history of exploring the ins and outs of poverty. In many ways, it is why the academic discipline exists in the first place.

Most of what I read on poverty in college was focused on underdeveloped countries overseas. You could even go so far as to say that this book was written, in part, out of a secret jealousy of economist Paul Collier. As a thirty-two-year-old college student, with a wife, three boys, and a mortgage, I knew I would not be spending any semesters abroad, nor would I be pursuing any academic careers trekking across the globe. Due to circumstances, I had to look to my own backyard to be part of the study of poverty.

If this book has been even a quarter as interesting and thought-provoking as one of Collier's works, then I will consider the time writing it well-spent. If my modest story inspires you, like Collier, Sachs, and Duflo have inspired me, then I will consider my time writing it to have been extremely profitable. I hope you see this study as a humble entrance into a much greater conversation about poverty.

Before I type "the end," let me take a moment to thank you for joining me at the exit ramp. I hope that I answered a few of the questions you had and that I left you with many more. More than that, I hope you are just a bit better equipped to be truly and effectively charitable. Generosity is a virtue that I consider to be deeply embedded in the DNA of what it means to be an American. After all, over a hundred-and-eighty-seven people proved that to me last summer.

THE END

# SPECIAL THANKS

Thanks to the Kickstarter community for helping make this book possible, with especial thanks to the following individuals:

Marta Grunsky

Martha Newman

Dot McQuade

Ken Houghton

Aaron Kulbe

Eric Dau

Paul Stoos

Karla Lortz

Kevin DeGraaf

www.ingramcontent.com/pod-product-compliance
Lightning Source LLC
Chambersburg PA
CBHW060631210326
41520CB00010B/1561